"THE GALLANT SIMS"
A CIVIL WAR HERO REDISCOVERED

NC

Antietam

Fitz-ry

CAPTAIN SAMUEL SIMS

"THE GALLANT SIMS"
A CIVIL WAR HERO REDISCOVERED

BY

Jeffrey I. Richman

THE GREEN-WOOD HISTORIC FUND

BROOKLYN, NEW YORK

2016

Furthermore:
a program of the J.M.Kaplan Fund

This publication is made possible by a grant provided
by Furthermore: a program of the J. M. Kaplan Fund.

COVER:

Samuel Sims, 1860 or 1861. The mount to this carte de
visite photograph is marked "Gurney & Son/Photo NY."
That firm was formed in 1860. Sims wears a militia
uniform here, likely dating this image no later than
1861. By the time of his service in the 51st New York
Volunteer Infantry, late in 1861, he would have been
wearing a standard issue Union Army officer's uniform.

INTRODUCTION

I N APRIL OF 1861, as the Civil War began, Samuel Harris Sims, a 32-year-old Brooklyn glass stainer, enlisted in the 13th New York State Militia as a second lieutenant to fight to preserve the Union. He served three months in Maryland with the 13th, most of it in uniform but some of it acting as a spy in Baltimore. Discharged, he almost immediately re-enlisted in the 51st New York Volunteers, recruiting and commanding its Company G. For the next three years, Sims led his men into some of the major battles of the war, serving in North Carolina, Virginia, Tennessee, Kentucky, and Mississippi, but periodically returning to New York to recruit more volunteers. All the while he exchanged letters with his fiancée, Carrie Dayton, to whom he sent Virginia wildflowers and a Mississippi passion flower, as well as his sister, his mother, his three children, and friends. Sims, a professional artist, drew what he saw during his service and skillfully carved peach pits as tokens of his love.

On July 27, 1864, after three years of service, Captain Sims, knowing that he would soon be leading the right wing of his regiment forward in the impending full front attack, wrote from Petersburg, Virginia, that "there will be stirring times . . . I am fully conscious of what might happen to me." Three days later, he was killed at the Battle of the Crater. His comrades soon retrieved his body and buried it on the field; he was interred at Brooklyn's Green-Wood Cemetery 17 days after his death. Major John G. Wright of the 51st wrote from Virginia about the loss of the regiment's senior captain: "He was an officer of sterling abilities, and he leaves behind him a reputation untarnished, which, with his fine social qualities, has endeared his memory to all his surviving comrades."

But the story of Samuel Sims was not over with his burial. Memories of him survived: soon after the Civil War ended, the men who had served in battle with "The Gallant Sims," as they called him, took up a collection to pay for his daughter's college education; she became "The Daughter of the Regiment." In 1880, the Confederate who had captured Captain Sims's sword when he was killed returned it to his family. In 1886, a soldier who had served with Sims was walking across the grounds of Brooklyn's Green-Wood Cemetery when he came across Sims's grave. Distressed that there was no appropriate monument there, he began a campaign to raise funds for one. The monument that was unveiled in 1888, paid for by the men who had served with Sims, described him as "The Gallant Sims" and as "Our Comrade." Inscribed on the four sides of its obelisk are the names of the many battles Sims fought in. And this was carved in the granite: "In Life We Esteemed This Valiant Soldier, In Death We Honor Him."

Two families, the descendants of his fiancée and his own, preserved many of the objects and documents that now make it possible for this book to tell Captain Sims's story. In 1976, a descendant came across Sims's papers and objects that Carrie Dayton, Sims's fiancée, had lovingly saved. And, in 1993, after Captain Sims's grandson's widow died in California without heirs, Captain Sims's commissions, letters, drawings, and personal possessions were unceremoniously put out for trash collection. Fortunately, they were rescued at the last minute and Green-Wood now owns many of these items from both collections.

Together, these objects and documents tell a fascinating story of love, patriotism, art, war, camaraderie, and more.

This is the story of a good and great man – "patriot, hero, martyr," Samuel Harris Sims.

NOTES

Though many 19th century amateur writers were good at turning a phrase, spelling was not their strong suit. So, in order to aid the reader, many spelling errors have been corrected in the pages that follow – though a few are so quirky that they have been left as is. Abbreviations in letters and reports have been expanded into complete words to make reading easier.

Thanks to Furthermore for helping to fund the publication of this book. And thanks to Green-Wood's Lisa Alpert and Melissa Levinsohn for their great work on the Furthermore grant application. As always, it has been a great pleasure to work with Jerry Kelly on this book design. Jerry is a true professional. And thanks to Stacy Locke, Green-Wood's manager of collections, for all of her help, including fine photographs of items in The Green-Wood Historic Fund Collections. Karen Daly's careful editing is very gratefully acknowledged. I am grateful to Gregory Di Salvio, who found the pair of carte de visite photographs of Samuel Sims and what may be his wife that appear in this book. I also acknowledge the contributions of James Lambert, volunteer extraordinaire, who created the Sims family tree, and Archigrafika, which mapped Captain Sims's assignments during the Civil War. Many many thanks to Joan Teshima who, as always, is a great help and comfort.

Finally, thanks to Sue Ramsey, who, by her own account, has fallen in love with Captain Sims. Sue has done everything in her power – transcribing letters, contacting descendants, handing out CDs of images and documents of Captain Sims – to keep his story alive. Years ago I told her someday I would write a book telling his story. This is that book.

Mark Curry, recently.

CHAPTER 1

Picking "Trash" In Santa Barbara, California

B Y ALL APPEARANCES, it would be a typical day on the job for Mark Curry. But then it wasn't.

Mark Curry had been working for the Southern California Gas Company for years. On March 23, 1993, all seemed routine. He even recognized the address he had been assigned to that day for execution of a close order: 2122 East Valley Road in the wealthy Ortega Ridge section of picturesque Santa Barbara, California. He remembered the elderly woman – Dorothy Sims – who had lived there; he had been to her home several times to hook up a stove. But this time would be different – she had died and his task was now a simple one: turn off the gas.

As Curry walked up the driveway towards the house, he saw workers there, stripping sheetrock from the walls. The house was being gutted – perhaps it had been sold. Curry would not have to go into the house; the meter was in a vault back at the road, and that's where he did the job. Mission accomplished. But for some reason he glanced over at the nearby trash cans. As he did so, he could hear the garbage truck approaching – it was perhaps two houses away. And, as he looked again, he saw what looked like old papers in scrapbooks. Intrigued, he grabbed them and put them in his truck.

Because Mark Curry did so, we today can better tell the story of Captain Samuel Harris Sims – the man whom his Civil War comrades called "The Gallant Sims" – who died at the Battle of the Crater almost 129 years before that day in 1993.

It was not until that night, when Curry got home, that it

began to dawn on him what he had rescued. There were letters, written from Virginia and Kentucky and other places during the Civil War. There were military commissions. There were drawings.

Mark threw himself into his find. He read about the 51st New York Volunteer Infantry, the regiment in which this Captain Sims had served. He bought some related artifacts and did some more research. Six years after his find, in 1999, he sold the precious papers that he had found in the trash.

How had these papers, so much a part of the Sims family for three generations and more than a century, wound up in the garbage, then been saved in a nick of time?

In fact, the Sims family had long recognized Sam's legacy – and the importance of this cache. The Sims papers had passed from Captain Samuel Harris Sims to his brother Palin, to Sam's son Samuel Austin Sims, and then to Sam's grandson Kenneth Hale Sims. All of these Simses had cherished them.

So what had gone wrong? How had these objects and papers made their way into trash cans, only to be saved, at the last minute, by a stranger, Mark Curry?

Kenneth Sims, Captain Sims's grandson and the son of Samuel A. Sims and Harriet King Sims, was born on August 27, 1899, in Minneapolis, Minnesota. On his Service Registration Card, filled out in 1918 when he was 19 years old, during World War I, he listed his occupation as a student in the Students' Army Training Corps (S.A.T.C.) and his employer as the United States Government at Fort Sheridan, Illinois. The S.A.T.C. was an officer procurement program for World War I staffing; the armistice soon after the program began ended it.

Kenneth attended the University of Minnesota and served as a staff sergeant in the Reserved Officers' Training Corps (ROTC). He played in the interfraternity tennis championship

THE SIMS FAMILY TREE

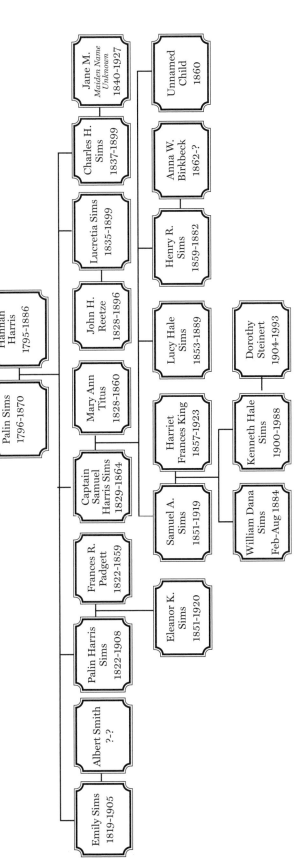

This tree shows Captain Sims's parents, siblings, in-laws, children, and grandchildren. It does not include other descendants.

Palin Sims
1796-1870

Hannah Harris
1795-1886

Emily Sims
1819-1905

Albert Smith
?-?

Palin Harris Sims
1822-1908

Frances R. Padgett
1822-1859

Captain Samuel Harris Sims
1829-1864

Mary Ann Titus
1828-1860

John H. Reetze
1828-1896

Lucretia Sims
1835-1899

Charles H. Sims
1837-1899

Jane M.
Maiden Name Unknown
1840-1927

Eleanor K. Sims
1851-1920

Samuel A. Sims
1851-1919

Harriet Frances King
1857-1923

Lucy Hale Sims
1853-1889

Henry R. Sims
1859-1882

Anna W. Birkbeck
1862-?

Unnamed Child
1860

William Dana Sims
Feb-Aug 1884

Kenneth Hale Sims
1900-1988

Dorothy Steinert
1904-1993

"The Gopher," the yearbook of the University of Minnesota, with its entry for Kenneth
Sims.

there in 1921, representing the fraternity Alpha Sigma Phi. He
and a fraternity brother won the doubles championship 6-3,
4-6, 7-5, 7-5. In 1921, the College of Science, Literature, and
the Arts awarded Kenneth Sims a Bachelor of Arts degree; he
graduated Phi Beta Kappa.

In 1922 and 1923, he was a faculty member at the university.
He then moved to New York City to work for General Motors in
its treasurer's department. There he met Dorothy Steinert. She
had been born in New York City in 1904, had attended Colby
College in Maine, and had graduated from Pratt Institute in
Brooklyn. In 1927, Kenneth and Dorothy married in New York
City. As the newspaper in Dobbs Ferry, New York, where her
parents lived, reported, "The wedding came as a surprise to the
many friends of the young couple."

In 1931, Kenneth became the treasurer of the Berwind-
White Coal Mining Company. He worked there until 1955,
when he retired and moved, with Dorothy, to Santa Barbara,
California. They bought their house, at 2122 East Valley Road,
just months after it was built, and Dorothy soon was attending a landscaping class. Together they spent the ensuing re-
tirement years laying out and planting the lovely gardens that
surrounded their house.

Five years after their arrival in Santa Barbara, Kenneth and
Dorothy took part in the Community Art Association's 1960

The Sims house, a California ranch, was of concrete block and glass; picture windows brought the outdoors inside, allowing them to enjoy their cherished gardens from both inside and outside their house.

A closer view of the house and patio.

Kenneth and Dorothy in their garden, May 1959. This is the caption to this photograph that appeared in the *Santa Barbara News-Press*: "Rewards of gardening are reflected in the happy faces of Mr. and Mrs. Kenneth Sims as they come down one of the small paths in their garden under the live oaks where they have a 'shady' garden. Apartment dwellers in the east for many years, neither one had ever gardened before undertaking the landscaping of their one-acre plot at 2122 E. Valley Road." Courtesy of the *Santa Barbara News-Press*.

garden tour for Fiesta Week, opening up what was described as their "charming garden" to the public. A local newspaper reported that "varied planting ranging from cactus to cymbidiums features the 'showplace garden of Mr. and Mrs. Kenneth Sims.'"

The report continued: "the couple had lived for years in apartments in the east and had never gardened before" but, trying their hands at gardening on their one acre lot, that had, in just three years, turned every inch of it into a place of "great beauty" and their "pride and joy." Live oaks had been there when they moved in; the fruit trees and shrubs that they planted had thrived in the year-round growing climate. Kenneth had put in a gravel path to reach one of their far-off plantings. The Simses had done all of the gardening themselves except for planting the lawn and a few shrubs. Their orchard included 20 avocado trees as well as lemons and limes. From their house and gardens were magnificent views of the mountains in the distance.

Kenneth, an enthusiastic gardener, was a member of the Santa Barbara Botanic Garden.

He also became an avid photographer and joined the Santa Barbara Color Camera Club.

When Kenneth died in 1988, his will left all of his property to his wife, Dorothy. They had had no children. If she predeceased him, equal shares of his estate were to go to the American Red Cross, the University of Minnesota, Colby College, the ASPCA, and the Santa Barbara Foundation (for the benefit of aged residents).

Dorothy Steinert Sims lived in their beloved home in Santa Barbara for five years after the death of her husband. She died on February 8, 1993, after an extended illness. In her will, she left her estate, as similarly specified in her late husband's will, equally to the five institutions listed above. In keeping with their wishes, no funeral services were held for either of them.

The land and house in which Kenneth and Dorothy had lived for years was appraised at $465,000. Household furniture and furnishings – the contents of the house – were appraised at a rather modest $1000. No mention was made in the appraisal of Captain Sims or his papers. The house was sold, within a few months of Dorothy's death, for the appraised value. Its interior was being gutted when Mark Curry came by to turn off the gas there – and rescued the items that were about to be picked up as garbage.

CHAPTER 2

Opening A Trunk In Poughkeepsie

IN THE SUMMER OF 1976, a teenage Stuart McPherson traveled to Poughkeepsie, New York, to spend a month with his grandmother, Ruth Taggart Stanley (1903-1977), and his great aunt, Estelle Taggart (1892-1984). They were sisters, the daughters of Lucius Baldwin Taggart (1857-1928) and Carrie Dayton Taggart (1869-1955).

As Stuart settled in, Great Aunt Estelle mentioned one day that there was something for him in her bedroom closet. He asked what; she replied that he would have to go and see. There on the floor was an object wrapped in brown paper and tied with string. Stuart unwrapped it and found the old carte de visite photograph album of her grandfather – Stuart's great great grandfather, Henry Birdsall Titus (1834-1893). Henry had married Josephine Adelia Dayton, sister of Augustus (known as Gus) Jehiel Dayton (1829-1897) and Caroline (known as Carrie) Eliza Dayton (1838-1911). Carte de visite photograph albums had been all the rage during the Civil War – a place to display your collection of photographs of your loved ones, the men you

Stuart McPherson at the commemoration ceremonies at Green-Wood on Memorial Day Weekend, 2007. It was to Stuart that Carrie Dayton's trunkful of objects, letters, and newspaper clippings concerning the life and death of her fiancé, Captain Samuel Sims, was passed.

Henry Birdsall Titus's photograph album. The Green-Wood Historic Fund Collections.

knew who were away at war, and the military and political heroes of the time. Among the photos in the album, some were identified in pencil; one of those was of a Captain Samuel Harris Sims.

Stuart was thrilled. He had been raised in a family that prized history and stories of his ancestors. He knew about four ancestors who had served in the Civil War: one of them died at Gettysburg, fighting for the Union, and that soldier's brother fought at that same battle for the Confederacy. Stuart also knew the story of his Great Aunt Carrie, his great grandmother's namesake, Carrie Dayton. She had been engaged to Captain Sims, but they never married because he was killed in battle during the Civil War.

Caroline Eliza Dayton was born on 162nd Street in New York City on June 23, 1838. Her mother was Adelia Malvinia Trowbridge Dayton (1808-1882). Her father, John Augustus Dayton (1805-1879), was a wealthy insurance man and real estate broker. He also was a political leader in Brooklyn, serving as an alderman, supervisor, on the board of education, and as a state legislator. As the Civil War approached, he chaired the War Committee of 1860, supporting the "boys in blue"; four of his sons fought for the Union.

By 1850, the Dayton family had moved to Brooklyn. Carrie grew up there, surrounded by a large family, including her parents and nine siblings. Their "spacious house" on Fulton Street was surrounded by extensive grounds that stretched for almost an entire city block. According to the 1855 New York State census, five servants were staffing the house. Carrie seems to have led a quiet life, living with family throughout her life and not working outside the home – typical for a well-off woman of the time. She was 26 years old when Captain Sims died; she never married. Throughout her life – both before and after the death of her fiancé, Captain Sims, she was on the lookout for any newspaper account pertaining to him, clipping and pasting

Group photograph, circa 1900, of Carrie Dayton with the Taggarts. From left to right, and from back to front, they are: Libbie, Aunt Ebeline (Carrie Dayton's sister), Carrie Dayton Taggart, Estelle, Charlie, Elizabeth, and Aunt Carrie Dayton (who had been affianced to Captain Sims).

whatever she found. By 1900, she was living in Mount Vernon, New York, with Lucius B. Taggart, his wife, Carrie Dayton Taggart, and their two daughters, Estelle (Stuart's Great Aunt Estelle) and Elizabeth.

According to the 1910 United States census, Carrie Dayton and the Taggarts were living in Manhattan. Carrie died on January 27, 1911, back in Brooklyn. Her funeral was held in Green-Wood Cemetery's then-just-opened (and now landmarked) chapel three days after her death. She was interred in lot 8275, where her parents already rested, almost half a century after Captain Sims's death.

By the 1970s, Stuart's Great Aunt Estelle was the oldest member of the family and its storyteller. Aunt Estelle well remembered her Aunt Carrie – Carrie Dayton – who was her grandmother's sister. Estelle and Carrie had lived together, with the Taggarts, for many years. Estelle knew Captain Sims's story well because she had heard it directly from Carrie. When Carrie died in 1911, Estelle was almost twenty years old.

The final resting place of Carrie Dayton, Captain Sims's fiancée. Her Green-Wood grave is unmarked.

ABOVE LEFT: The trunk that held the mementoes of Captain Sims that Carrie Dayton saved. The Green-Wood Historic Fund Collections.

ABOVE RIGHT: Peach pits, carved during the Civil War by Captain Samuel Sims for his fiancée, Carrie Dayton, as tokens of his love. They were found in the trunk. The Green-Wood Historic Fund Collections.

During Stuart's month-long stay with his ancestors, he helped out with chores around the house, doing yard work, painting, and helping to move heavy items around the basement storage area. Stuart discovered several old trunks down there and within a few days was able to convince Grandmother Ruth and Aunt Estelle to go back down and open them up. As they looked through the saved mementos, his grandmother and aunt told him about the items. In Aunt Estelle's trunk, which had been passed down by Henry Birdsall Titus, was a collection of items given to her by Great Aunt Carrie in 1910, the year before Carrie died; as Stuart has described them, "items of the greatest sentiment that tell of a loving remembrance that transcends time itself. Ever faithful to Sam's memory, she had carefully held on to these relics keeping them safe, perhaps in hopes to help tell the story as she instilled it in Aunt Estelle who in turn instilled it in me."

Stuart continues:

Among the items saved were two peach pits thought to be carved by Sam and given to Carrie, a single brass button and captain's shoulder board from his uniform, a letter he wrote with a flower enclosed and carried through battle, finishing [the letter] days later, stating he will honor his former promise of marriage. Also her ivory sheeted diary stating the date of her engagement and Sam's subsequent death; a black jet match safe and a small plaque of the 9th Army Corp Insignia showing

Carrie Dayton's ivory diary. It is opened to three entries: "Engaged Oct. 9th, 1863-"; "April 18th/64 Captain Sims went away for Annapolis"; "Captain Sims was killed before Petersburg to-day July 30th/64." The Green-Wood Historic Fund Collections.

anchor and cannon that Sims had designed himself. An oval mother of pearl, abalone, ivory and tortoise shell encased photo of Sam and another cdv [carte de visite photograph] of him also. Old newspaper clippings giving details about him and the movements of the regiment, but one of the most amazing items saved among the collection, to me, has always been the pieces of the Battle Flag of the 51st New York State Volunteers held within an envelope with Sam's hand written notation stating so. Oh to ever, one day, find more pieces so identified!

Gus Dayton, in his Civil War officer's uniform, circa 1863, and later in life.

The final resting place of Augustus Dayton at Green-Wood Cemetery. In addition to being a Civil War soldier and good friend of Captain Sims, Gus was also a star baseball player in Brooklyn, where the national pastime was incubated. Born in Brooklyn in 1829, he worked with his father in real estate, pitched and played the outfield for Brooklyn's Pastime Base Ball Club, served in the Civil War with Captain Sims in the 13th and 51st Regiments, then rose to the rank of captain in the 159th New York Infantry. After the war, Gus worked as a clerk, bookkeeper, and as a guard at Sing Sing Prison. In 1889, a Brooklyn newspaper reported that, retired, he had been "building model yachts the past year or two." He died in 1897.

Stuart was very proud of this Sims Collection, which was passed along to him by his Great Aunt Estelle a year after he had opened that trunk – in 1977 – in the wake of the bicentennial of the signing of the Declaration of Independence. He knew that not only had Captain Sims been his ancestor's fiancé, but also that Carrie's brother, Gus Dayton, was a very close friend of Sims and had served with him during the Civil War.

So, as Stuart tells it,

> I would often search looking for any further information to enhance my knowledge of the regiment and its particular members. Lo and behold there came up on eBay another letter written by Sims and I thought perhaps a collection may have been saved by a branch of his family and now, with the craze for original Civil War material, they began to sell off their family history. Further queries discovered quite a cache and strengthened my searching ever hoping to find more of the elusive letters from a collection slowly being scattered to the corners of the earth . . . .

As Stuart would learn, years after he was given Carrie Dayton's treasures by his Great Aunt Estelle, items from the Sims family collection, which had descended through Captain Sims's brother, son and grandson, and had been saved by Mark Curry in Santa Barbara, California, then passed through several dealers and were offered for sale. Stuart was able to buy many of those items and unite them with those that Carrie Dayton had saved. Stuart concludes that there must have been "an indescribable force that saved the collection in its separate components from being forever lost to oblivion. . . ."

CHAPTER 3

Falling in Love with Captain Sims – 130 Years After His Death

IN THE SUMMER OF 1994, a year after Mark Curry had rescued Captain Sims's papers from the garbage, he heard a fellow employee at the Southern California Gas Company talking about her upcoming trip to the East Coast to visit Civil War battlefields there. Mark approached Sue Ramsey and said something to the effect of, "I have some Civil War letters that you should read. I guarantee they will change your life." Mark was right; they did. As Sue puts it, "I did read the letters and fell instantly in love with Captain Samuel Sims." Mark allowed Sue to make copies of everything he had found.

Sue worked at organizing Mark's finds. Four years went by. In the fall of 1998, Sue attended a meeting of the Santa Barbara County Genealogical Society. The topic: the Civil War. Bob Duncan – a retired Marine sergeant who had served in the Korean War, a Civil War enthusiast, Commander of the General William T. Sherman Camp 28 of the Sons of Union Veterans of the Civil War, and leader of the effort to restore the Cieneguitas Civil War veteran's cemetery – was one of the speakers. Sue brought her Captain Sims material along. After the meeting she introduced herself to Bob and showed him her binder. He was excited after a quick look and borrowed the material. They talked soon thereafter and shared their enthusiasm for the material and Captain Sims's story. Subsequently, Bob helped get Sue involved in Civil War activities – reenactments, Civil War roundtable meetings, etc.

Sue Ramsey, who organized Captain Sims's papers and kept his memory alive.

In June 1999, Bob asked Sue if Mark Curry would be interested in selling his finds. He was. Sue, at Mark's request, acted as his go-between with the buyer – and Mark's discoveries – Captain Sims's papers – were sold.

Several months later, Sue learned that the buyer had kept a few of the sketches but had sent everything else off for auction. Various buyers wound up purchasing items.

As Sue notes,

This was early in my venture into the Civil War and I had no idea I would become so involved with Sam, his regiment, and the war in general. At this point in time, I only wanted to make copies of the collection should a family member emerge who would be interested. Had I known then what I know now, I would have purchased the collection myself. Yes, I kick myself regularly for my involvement in this sale.

In the fall of 2003, Sue found a query online concerning a soldier in the 51st New York. Dale Niesen of Michigan was looking for information on his great grand uncle, the Civil War veteran Peter Niesen. After corresponding with Dale and talking on the phone, he suggested they start a website to attract other people looking for information on the 51st. He would be the webmaster and Sue would field the queries. The site was launched in October 2003 – and is still active.

Shortly after the site went up, Stuart MacPherson, living in Connecticut, contacted Sue. His great grand aunt, Carrie Dayton, had been engaged to Samuel Sims during the war and he had many items from Sam that she had saved. Stuart also had purchased many of the Sims items Mark had found in Santa Barbara.

Sue, eager to share Sam's story, presented it to a genealogy class in Santa Barbara during the winter of 2004. She then wrote an article about Sam for *Ancestor's West*, Santa Barbara County Genealogical Society's quarterly magazine. Sue worked at transcribing Sam's letters and scanning the documents from her color laser copies. She then burned CDs of the images and transcriptions to distribute to others.

Early in July 2005, Sue came across an advertisement in *Civil War News* requesting information about Civil War soldiers buried at Green-Wood Cemetery in Brooklyn, New York. The ad, which had been posted by Jeff Richman, Green-Wood's historian who was leading its Civil War Project, gave his email address. Sue immediately sent Jeff an email telling him what she had. Jeff responded enthusiastically the next day and asked that she call him, which she did. He was, at that time, working on a book of letters written during the war by the Civil War veterans buried at Green-Wood. Sue sent him one of her CDs. Some of the Sims letters were incorporated into his book, *Final Camping Ground: Civil War Veterans at Brooklyn's Green-Wood Cemetery, in Their Own Words*, published in 2007.

As time went by, Sims descendants began to contact Sue. One of Palin Sims's great great grandsons, Rod DuCasse, reached her in March of 2006; she sent him CDs for himself and his siblings. Sue told Rod about the Green-Wood Civil War Project. He met with the cemetery historian, Jeff Richman, in May, and they went to the gravesite where the three Sims brothers who served in the Civil War, Sam, Palin, and Charlie, are interred. They discovered that only Sam, of the brothers, had a gravestone.

A few months later, Sue was contacted via *Ancestry.com* by Donna Mead, the great great granddaughter of Palin Sims. Sue had posted a correction to one of Donna's family trees. They hit it off immediately. Donna got one of the Samuel Sims CDs from Sue.

On Memorial Day weekend, 2007, Green-Wood hosted a Civil War commemoration. Sue flew in from California; she was joined at the cemetery by Donna Mead, Rod DuCasse, and other Sims descendants. Sue and Green-Wood's historian, Jeff Richman, met for the first time.

During the ceremonies at Green-Wood, descendants of the Civil War veterans interred there, who had traveled to Brooklyn from across the country and around the world, read the names of their ancestors. Rod read Palin's name, Donna read Charlie's, and Sue read Sam's. Stuart MacPherson, who had inherited Carrie Dayton's collection, was there with his daughter, Annie. He mentioned to Sue that he was thinking about selling his collection of Samuel Sims items.

After this ceremony, all of those there to honor the Sims brothers went to Sam's grave. Sue placed a wreath there. She was very moved to finally be at his grave.

Soon thereafter, Stuart decided to sell his collection. It was difficult for Stuart to part with it. However, he wanted it to remain intact and felt that transferring it to Green-Wood would be the best thing to do. So, in 2007, the Sims Collection – a combination of the items saved by Carrie Dayton, then passed on through her family, and those saved by the Sims descendants and rescued by Mark Curry, became the property of The Green-Wood Historic Fund.

Sue concludes:

> In the subsequent years, I have given several talks about Sam and my journey with him. I've given talks at genealogy meetings, Daughters of Union Veterans of the Civil War meetings, church

groups, Rotary groups, and one retiree group. I have expanded my knowledge of the Civil War exponentially through reading, touring battlefields, various group involvements, etc. I have also become more involved with the Civil War Project at Green-Wood and have continued to research other Civil War veterans buried there. I am currently starting my 9th year as president of Laura Belle Stoddard, Tent 22, Daughters of Union Veterans of the Civil War, 1861-1864 in Santa Barbara.

None of these things would have happened without my introduction to Captain Samuel Sims. Mark was correct when he said reading those letters would change my life!!!

These gravestones, obtained by Green-Wood's Civil War Project about 10 years ago, now mark the formerly-unmarked graves of Captain Sims's brothers – Palin and Charlie – who served during the war. They are next to Captain Sims's Green-Wood monument.

Inside the Broadway Tabernacle Church, where Samuel Harris Sims and Mary Ann Titus were married in 1850.

CHAPTER 4

Samuel Harris Sims,
Before and Early in the Civil War

BORN IN 1829 in New York City, Samuel Harris Sims was one of the five children of Palin and Hannah Sims, both of whom were natives of Leicester, England. Sam had four siblings: Emily Sims (born 1819), Palin Harris Sims (born 1822), Lucretia Sims (born 1830), and Charles Harris Sims (born 1837).

Sam was 5' 9" tall with a light complexion, brown hair and blue eyes. He was educated at what were then called common schools – now referred to as public schools. On September 12, 1850, he married Mary Ann Titus in New York City, "according to the ordinance of God and the laws of this State." Pastor Joseph P. Thompson of the Broadway Tabernacle Church officiated.

Sam and Mary Ann had three children: Samuel Austin, born in 1851, Lucy Hale, born in 1853, and Henry Ridgewood, born in 1859.

According to the Brooklyn City Directory of 1859, Sam was working as a glass stainer – painting on glass to create decorative windows – at 322 Atlantic Avenue and living nearby, at 256 Bergen Street, with his family. His employer was glass stainer Henry Bloor. William Vidler Bloor, Henry's brother, also worked there. Sims and the Bloors were close; when William Bloor, an English immigrant, applied in 1860 in Brooklyn's City Court to become a naturalized citizen, Sam signed his petition as his witness. Sam swore, in the application, that Bloor "was a man of good moral character – sincerely attached to the principles of the Constitution and the forms of government of the United States of America, and the good order and happiness of the same."

Details of carte de visite photographs of Samuel Sims, and what may be his wife Mary Ann, circa 1860. These photographs, labeled on their mounts as by the photographer Sherman of Brooklyn, were recently identified as of, and associated with, Samuel Sims. One has "S. Sims" and "80" written in pencil on its back; the other, of the woman, has "Sims" and "81" penciled on its back. Based on a comparison with the identified photograph of Samuel Sims in his captain's uniform that appears on page of this book, these are both photographs of the same man. And, given that the numbers on the backs are consecutive, the photograph of the woman is associated with that of Samuel Sims. Though it might be one of Sam's sisters, or even a sister-in-law, the likelihood is that he and his wife dressed up in their finest to have these pictures taken. The Green-Wood Historic Fund Collections.

Sam was long active in the military. In May 1846, he was promoted to corporal of the 13th Regiment, New York State Militia. In April 1851, "in the seventy-fifth year of the Independence of the United States of America," he enlisted as a private in Company D of the 14th Regiment of the New York State Militia. On September 3 of that same year, he was promoted to corporal: "You are to obey the orders which you shall, from time to time, receive from your superior officers, and to discharge the duty of CORPORAL in said company, with fidelity, according to the laws and regulations established for the government and discipline

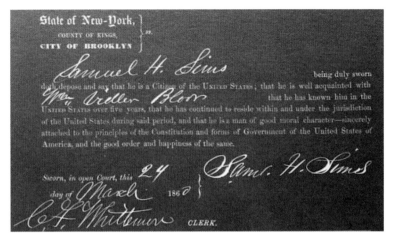

Samuel H. Sims's signed statement, given in 1860, in support of the application of his boss's brother, William Vidler Bloor, for citizenship. The language of this document foreshadows the deadly struggle that would begin only a year later, over "the principles of the Constitution and the forms of government of the United States of America," and in which 750,000 lives, including that of Samuel Sims, would be lost.

Samuel Harris Sims's commission as a first lieutenant in the 14th New York State Militia, dated June 27, 1859. The Green-Wood Historic Fund Collections.

of the Militia of this State." In March 1858, he was promoted to sergeant. Governor Edwin Morgan, on behalf of the "People of the State of New York, By the Grace of God Free and Independent," commissioned Sims a first lieutenant in June 1859.

On December 7, 1860, Mary Ann Sims, Sam's wife and the mother of their three young children, died of anemia at their Bergen Street residence. This likely was the result of complications from childbirth; an unnamed "child of Mr. Sims" (as it was recorded in cvemetery records), address 256 Bergen Street, was stillborn on November 14, 1860, and had been interred at Green-Wood less than a month earlier. Mary Ann, just 32 years old, was interred at Green-Wood Cemetery within days of her death.

Soon after the first shots of the Civil War were fired, at Fort Sumter in Charleston Harbor, South Carolina, on April 12, 1861, Samuel Harris Sims answered the call of President Abraham

Samuel Harris Sims, in his militia uniform, likely around the time of the beginning of the Civil War. The Green-Wood Historic Fund Collections.

Lincoln for troops to protect the nation's capital, Washington, D.C. Sam enlisted as a second lieutenant in Company B of the 13th Regiment, New York State Militia, on April 23, 1861, to serve three months and to fight to preserve the Union.

The 13th, part of the first wave of militia hastily dispatched to defend the nation's capital, consisted of eight companies when it left New York State on the 23rd. Sims left his three young children in the care of his sister, Lucretia Sims.

Colonel Abel Smith was in command of the 13th Regiment as it proceeded south. It was mustered into the service of the United States and served as infantry at Annapolis and Baltimore, Maryland. Sam wrote from the Maryland capital to his mother:

ANNAPOLIS, MARYLAND
JUNE 15, 1861

Dear Mother,

We are "under orders" to proceed to "Locust Point" near Baltimore. The object I do not know. We understand that we leave Annapolis for good. From present appearances there will be but little sleep in our camp tonight; as preparation to make our final move gives everyone a little trouble to dispose of the many things which have accumulated. The strict discipline of the camp is altogether upset in the hurry and confusion. I suppose we shall have rough times for a little while as all our nice "mess" arrangements will be broken up and we may have to come down to "soldiers fare" again.

But I welcome anything but inaction and will take my chance cheerfully no matter what turns up – so that we can strike for the cause. Still I do not apprehend anything that would cause you to be alarmed for me supposing for an instant that you have been any way anxious. Baltimore no doubt contains ugly customers, but I have full faith that while we lay near there they will not attempt to cut up any capers for we have gained something of a name beside we are to have a sufficient force to maintain our position against any force which could be brought against us from Baltimore.

As I informed you in my last letter, our regiment went on to Baltimore the day before yesterday. They had a quiet time no outbreak occurring from the election. They returned yesterday at noon. After the regiment left Annapolis the small guard left behind had a busy time to secure the garrison from a surprise. I had all the colored servants on duty and their readiness to fight any secessionists bold enough to think of taking advantage of our small force, gave us a good deal of fun.

The vote in the city gave a large majority for the <u>Union</u> candidate much to everybody's surprise. This afternoon the triumph was celebrated by raising a flag in the city, the troops parading through the town and taking part in the ceremony. Governor Hicks, Major General [Nathaniel] Banks, and others made speeches and all passed off quiet. So this part of Maryland is <u>safe</u> for <u>Union</u> and <u>order</u>.

All your letters (and I expect a good many) may be directed as heretofore until I advise you of our destination. They will be forwarded to our regiment from this place.

Let Mr. William & Henry Bloor know that I have not forgotten them. I will write them when we get to our next camp and trust to have something interesting to relate.

With love to all and kisses to the children whom I soon hope to see.

Your affectionate son,
Sam

Though absent from his civilian job as an artist in glass, Samuel Sims continued, while a soldier, to create art. Man on a donkey, pencil sketch by Samuel Harris Sims, made during the Civil War. Green-Wood Historic Fund Collection.

CAMP MORGAN, GALLOWS HILL,
BALTIMORE, MARYLAND
JULY 3, 1861

Dear Sister Lucretia,

Your letter of June 30th arrived here this morning and gave me great satisfaction for I have had no word for a long time. The letter from Sammy [Captain Sims's oldest child] also pleased me much.

. . . .

Since leaving Annapolis we have changed our encampment three times and we have had no easy times as you may suppose. It has been a continual round of duty with considerable discomfort in every shape yet the men endure it pretty well although a few grumblers see fit to write letters to the newspapers charging the whole as a fault of our Colonel. There is no doubt a good deal of inefficiency chargeable to officers but the reports we have read in Brooklyn and New York papers are abominable and their inferences are false and outrageous. We are now (a detachment of six companies) quartered in an old building situated on "Gallows Hill." The place is in the midst of the hot bed of secessionists and overlooks the whole city. You must be aware that Baltimore this last week has been occupied in every important part by the troops. The people are very bitter against us but the influence of our occupying the city has had the effect of giving confidence to the Union men as against the secessionists.

I have been employed in secret services the last ten days and at present have to keep close to my quarters. The information I have been able to procure has been of good service and gained me some compliment from General [Nathaniel] Banks.

I make a very good spy and have been deep in the confidence of the rebels so much so that they have entrusted communications to me intended for their friends in "Dixie" where of course I was to deliver them but I "forgot" and handed them to Genl. Banks who saw fit to benefit himself of the contents. I have two suits of clothes for my operations and you would not know me in them.

Tomorrow will be the Fourth of July and preparations are making in the city to celebrate the great day. Our men are to be allowed no liberty outside of quarters and with empty pockets and poor rations and miserable accommodations I am afraid that we shall have but little enjoyment other than the consciousness of doing our duty will bring.

It is said that we shall be paid soon. If so, it will accommodate us exactly. Our regiment has spent more money for necessities than all the pay will amount to especially among the privates where pay is but a trifle.

Our term of service expires on the 23rd of this month and then home again! If things remain, or obtain quiet in Baltimore – I do not doubt that will be at home near or about that time.

I hasten to close for the mail.

Your affectionate brother.
With love to all
Sam

On August 6, 1861, Sims and the 13th, having completed their service, were discharged at Brooklyn. His discharge, signed by Colonel Smith, noted that "No objection to his being re-enlisted is known to exist."

Sam was far from finished with the Civil War. Just ten days after his discharge from the 13th, Sims re-enlisted as a private in the 51st New York Volunteer Infantry. He signed his name as the first enlistee in Company G, gave his age as 33 years old, his address as 256 Bergen Street, Brooklyn, his occupation as glass stainer, and his nativity as New York City. His signing as the first enlistee in Company G was not mere happenstance; Sims was intent on recruiting a full company of 100 men from his comrades who had served with him in the 13th Regiment. Of the first 19 men who signed up in Company G with Sims, over the next two days, every one of them had served with him in the 13th Regiment. According to a history of the 13th Regiment, published in the *Brooklyn Daily Eagle* on February 17,

No.	Date of Enlistment.	Names.	Age.	Residence.
1	August 15	Saml. H. Sims	33	356 Bergen St Brooklyn
2	" 16	Augustus J. Dayton	32	301 Adelphia Brooklyn
3	16	William Robertson	29	102 Carlton av Brooklyn
4	" 16	Fr S Schoonmaker	21	69 Nassau St Brooklyn
5	16	John Wachmuth	25	Brooklyn
6	16	Lewis H. Baker	23	Brooklyn
7		Engaged Miller		
8	1 "	Andrew Cook	26	Putnam av co Bedford Brooklyn
9	16	Edw. L. Crooker	19	186 Livingston St Brooklyn
10	16	Charles H Ball	26	Brooklyn Myrtle Av
11	17	Joseph Carter	21	do
12				
13	" 17	P D Jellison	21	232 Fulton St Brooklyn
14	17.	John A. Galvin	21	401. Dean St. Brooklyn
15	Sept 3	Patrick Colgan	22.	Nutter St
16	17	Charles H. Wright	21	207 Livingston Brooklyn
17	17	Daniel Cox	21	259 Hudson av Brooklyn
18	17	F B Mc Grady	22	115 Brooklyn
19	17	Phillip Webber	26	N Brooklyn
20.	"	Henry Duhtorf	20	Cr Hudson and Fulton Brooklyn

Samuel Sims signature on the 51st 's enlistment sheet. The text at top reads: "We the undersigned whose names are affixed hereto, each for himself do hereby Enlist in Company – under and according to the above order, and agree to serve the United States Government faithfully under the Officers until discharged according to law." The enlistee right after Sims was Augustus J. Dayton –Sam's good friend Gus, whose sister Carrie Eliza Dayton was engaged to marry the widower Sims. The Green-Wood Historic Fund Collections.

State of New-York,

DEPOT OF VOLUNTEERS,

(Division Armory, cor. White and Elm Streets.)

New-York, Sept 20th 1861.

We, the undersigned Examiners, appointed for the New-York Depot of Volunteers, do hereby certify that we have examined

Saml. H. Sims

in the School of the Soldier and Company, and find him duly qualified to serve as a Company Officer.

[signatures of Examiners]

Samuel Sims's certification that he had been duly examined and was qualified to be an officer in the Union army. The Green-Wood Historic Fund Collections.

1864, his effort was a success, ". . . nearly one company of the 51st Regiment Volunteers, Capt. Sims, being raised of members of the 13th." This reenlistment by men who had served briefly at the outset of the Civil War was not unusual; as the same article notes, of the 1099 men who served with the 13th early in the Civil War, more than half subsequently re-enlisted in other regiments to continue their fight for the Union.

When it became apparent, after the first big battle of the Civil War, known as Bull Run or Manassas, that this conflict would not end with a single decisive battle, but rather only after a prolonged struggle, manpower changes had to be made. Terms of enlistments were extended – no longer 30 or 90 days, but for two or three years or even for the duration of the war. And officers had to be screened – it would no longer be enough that an officer, with little or no military training, had been elected by the popular vote of his men. Now it would be necessary to train and test officers – to determine that they were qualified to lead men into battle.

On September 10, after Samuel Sims had successfully recruited the soldiers of Company G of the 51st, he was promoted to captain and given command of those men. Ten days later, on September 20, 1861, he was examined at the School of Soldiers and Company, located at the New York Depot of Volunteers, White and Elm Streets in lower Manhattan, by two colonels. They judged him "duly qualified to serve as a Company Officer."

Soon Captain Samuel Harris Sims would be leading the men of Company G, 51st New York Volunteer Infantry, off to war and into battle. He would remain a captain for the rest of his service with the 51st – rejecting any and all promotions out of loyalty to his men of Company G – for the three years that remained of his life.

Map of where Captain Samuel Sims's served during the Civil War. Map by Archigrafika.

Off to War

O N OCTOBER 22, 1861, as the 51st New York Volunteer
Infantry undertook its final preparations before heading
off to the theater of war, Captain Samuel Sims led a contingent
of 100 men – likely all of his Company G – to the funeral of
Colonel Abel Smith, under whom Sims had served just weeks
earlier in the 13th Regiment. As the *Brooklyn Daily Eagle* reported, Smith "fell in the prime of his manhood and in the commencement of a career, in which he gave promise to shine with
brilliancy in the future pages of his country's history. But the
thread of life was cut short, and he has gone to his rest . . . ." It
was still early in the Civil War, when deaths and funerals were
rare, and so, even though Smith had died in a railroad accident,
and not in battle, thousands of civilians and hundreds of military men, as well as a detachment of police, the Navy Yard band,
and the band and drums corps of the 7th New York State Militia,
gathered at the late colonel's home. They then proceeded to the
Cemetery of the Evergreens for burial, where "the soldier was
left to his rest."

Just one week later, on October 29, the 51st Regiment, with
850 men under arms, left New York, arriving at Annapolis,
Maryland, the state capital, for guard duty and training. Danger lurked nearby. The city of Baltimore, just a few miles away,
was evenly split between Unionists and Confederate sympathizers; it was a dangerous place for Union troops. Of the 30,000
votes cast there for President in the election of 1860, Repub-
lican Abraham Lincoln had received only 1,100. On April 19,
1861, the 6th Massachusetts Militia had been attacked on the

streets of Baltimore as it marched between railroad terminals on its way to defend Washington, D.C. Four soldiers and 12 civilians were killed. Lincoln knew that, if Maryland joined the Confederacy, Washington would be surrounded by Confederate states and cut off from the North. So, on May 13, Union forces began to enforce martial law in Maryland. President Abraham Lincoln soon had local authorities arrested and imprisoned, without trial. And thousands of Union troops were garrisoned in Baltimore, to prevent further trouble.

Flank marker of the 51st New York State Volunteer Infantry. Courtesy of the New York State Military Museum.

CAMP BURNSIDE
ANNAPOLIS, MARYLAND
(LIKELY NOVEMBER) 1861

Dear Sister Lucretia,

I suppose that you have been worried a good deal at my not writing to you; but you will forgive me when I tell you that I could not get any favorable time to do so.

We are now encamped about 1½ miles from the Naval Academy – in an open field. There are four Massachusetts regiments surrounding us, who have come in since our arrival and are intended for the same brigade with us. It is likely that we shall remain some time to get in good shape.

I am anxious to know how you are getting along but trust that you will be able to make ends meet until "pay day" which I expect will arrive very soon.

There is nothing to relate of interest to you, that I could write, excepting that I am in good health and have got things in shape here to suit me. My company was selected to lay out the camp and we have satisfied everybody in the Regt with our plan and when they marched in after we had been on the ground two days in a drenching rain and wind storm they were surprised and delighted and gave us "three cheers."

The naval expedition which has gone south somewhere was a good part started from this place. Colonel [James] Perry's

Colonel Edward Ferrero was much admired by the men who served under his command in the 51st. However, after promotion to brigadier general, his incompetence at the Battle of the Crater cost many lives. He is interred at Green-Wood Cemetery. The Green-Wood Historic Fund Collections.

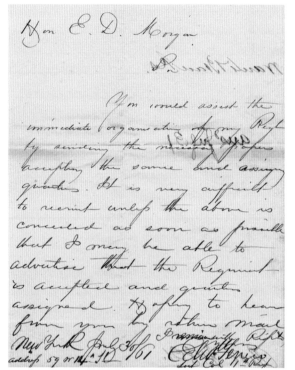

Letter from Edward Ferrero to the governor of New York State, asking his help in organizing the Shepard Rifles. Ferrero had had some militia experience, but his primary claim to fame, at this time, was as the dance instructor for West Point cadets. The Green-Wood Historic Fund Collections.

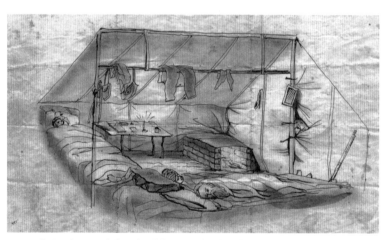

Samuel Sims's pencil sketch of the tent that he shared with two other officers at Camp Burnside, Maryland. The Green-Wood Historic Fund Collections.

regiment [the 48ᵗʰ New York Infantry, nicknamed "Perry's Saints" because he was a minister] is with them. The first day of our arrival we were encamped on the ground that they left.

Palin [Sam's older brother, who also had enlisted in the 51ˢᵗ] is getting along very well. He has got good quarters and enjoys himself very well. He always calls me Captain Sims.

The guard has just called out to have my lights extinguished "if I please." As I cannot help myself, I must obey the rules of the camp and "douse the glim." So dear Sister do not fret the least about me. I will take care of you and the dear ones at home and serve as a soldier too. I looked for you the day of our departure but was disappointed. However, let the daguerreotype be sent to me as soon as you can. I suppose Charly [Sam's youngest brother] is married by this time. Give him my best wishes also to his wife. Remember me to all who inquire to Mrs. Bloor also to William and Henry Bloor [Sam's employers in the glass staining business]. I wish I could have my light for I feel just like setting up all night to write. Kiss my little darlings for me. I hope they will appreciate your kind care of them. However I do; and it will be my earnest prayer that you may be blessed for it.

Good night and best love to you from your Affectionate Brother
Samuel

Keep the best care of mother give to her my love.

CAMP BURNSIDE, MARYLAND
DECEMBER 5, 1861

Dear Sister Lucretia,

Your letter came to hand yesterday, and I was glad to hear from you. Palin received a letter today, I believe from Mother. I am sorry to hear that she is not very well. You must keep in good spirits for all is going well with us, and also for the cause for which we are enrolled.

My health is excellent. I weigh ten pounds more than when I left home. Palin also looks better than I ever saw him. There has been a good deal of sickness in our camp on account of the bad weather.

Almost every day of the month of November was wet and our camp being pitched on level ground, the water does not drain well.

There is nothing occurring more than the ordinary routine of camp life. We cannot tell when the "division" of General [Ambrose] Burnside will leave Annapolis for the South. Some seem to think it will, about the first of January others think it will be "all winter" at Annapolis. So you see there is no certainty about it. I would rather start soon than lay all winter in this bleak place.

The last few days have been fine with frosty nights and a few more such days will make all the soldiers in hospital well. There has been much cause for complaint in the regiment for want of blankets sufficient also the want of rubber blankets. This want will soon be remedied and then our equipment is complete.

Palin has had his hands full attending to the "hard cases" in setting them to work and keeping them at it. He does well with them and gives satisfaction to the Colonel [Edward Ferrero] and the result is that we have perfect order in camp.

Lieutenant Cuff, Lieutenant Barker and myself occupy one tent about eleven feet square shaped like a small house thus (sketch of a tent). We have a colored boy to cook for us and he gets up good dinners too. We have apple dumplings, oysters, chicken pot pie and everything first rate. Lieut. Barker gets a box of varieties from home every week or so. We can't complain of lack in good eating but the case I suppose will be different when we leave. A sample of condensed coffee was shown us yesterday which is already sweetened and has milk in it. The government has adopted it for the use of those regiments who wish it. It is very good and I think it will be adopted, for a cup of good coffee, is a rarity in camp and nothing tastes better. The quality of all the provisions furnished for us, is better than that issued at the commencement of the war.

My time is taken up pretty well. The days are short and there is but little interval between the various duties. Our tent is heated by a small stove which makes it very comfortable for us. A friend of mine, Mr. McKee, came on to Annapolis and took dinner with us Thanksgiving day. We had roast turkey and all the "fixings."

. . . I am looking for letters from Sammy and Lucy [the oldest two of Sam's three children]. I would like it if I could let you hear my footsteps coming down the alley but at present I must not think of it. Give kisses to the children for me. I trust they are behaving well. They must for I could not bear to hear they were doing otherwise. Remember me to Charley [Sam's brother] and his wife. I have not answered Charley's letter yet. Remember me to Messrs. Bloor and their wives. Also to Mrs. Cruikshank and family. I must close for it gets late. Write soon

From your affectionate brother
Samuel

The 51st Regiment soon was assigned to Brigadier General Ambrose Burnside's North Carolina Expedition. The goal: take control of the sounds along the coast of North Carolina, cutting off that state's sea access and tightening the Union's blockade of the South. On January 6, 1862, the 51st left its camp at Annapolis, Maryland, and boarded ships, bound for Roanoke Island, North Carolina, to join naval forces and other infantry regiments in the attack on the Confederate forces there.

CAMP BURNSIDE
ANNAPOLIS, MARYLAND
JANUARY 5, 1862

Dear Sister Lucretia,

Your letter of Dec. 31st came to hand.

I have sent by "Adams Express" today, a package containing one hundred and eighty dollars. You may possibly receive the package before you get this letter.

You must write as soon as you get it, as I have remarked in my letter containing the money. Palin has sent thirty dollars to mother.

Tomorrow morning our regiment is to go on board the gunboats "Lancer" and "Pioneer." My company will be on board the first named.

Tonight will be a busy one for us. The men have to pack their knapsacks and fill their haversacks with "rations" for four days.

The vessels prepared for us are the finest of the fleet.

My second lieutenant has been appointed one of the "signal officers" for the expedition; his name is William H. Barker. He did not wish to leave my company although his appointment was an advancement.

My men are all in good health and spirits and I guess, take us altogether, we can manage to do our duty.

It is most likely that we shall remain on board some time, before the expedition moves to its destination. We may possibly lay at "Fortress Monroe." I have heard that there is to be thirty thousand more men to join us there.

I wish you to send Charley to Newark and let him pay Mr. John J. Read the amount of interest, due on Nov. 1st 1861 $52.50 (fifty-two dollars and fifty-cents). Let Charley get a receipt and be careful to preserve it. The next interest will be due on May 1st. I also wish that Charley would get insurance on the house from the Fireman's Insurance Company, opposite the City Hall, Brooklyn. I am acquainted with the secretary, Mr. Wm. Burrell.

There is a bill I owe to Mr. Charles Markham. He is a portrait painter and his place is in, I think, Pacific Street near Court [Street], Brooklyn. [Markham (1837-1907) was a New York City painter known for his cityscapes, still lifes and genre scenes. He was a member of the Brooklyn Art Association and exhibited at the National Academy of Design]. The house stands back from the street. The amount is about six dollars.

I shall take measures to send you eighty dollars per month from my pay. The pay day comes every two months so the next will be March 1st.

I suppose now I must close by saying that I realize fully all the risks I have undertaken. I do not think I am rash or impetuous. It appears to me now that I shall remain as cool as anybody could should we be put under heavy fire. However I do not feel any great dread.

You will direct your letters as usual until you hear of us from the destination of "Burnsides expedition." All letters will be forwarded to us from Annapolis, should any arrive there.

Sammy must get the "Times" and "Brooklyn Eagle" and read all about us. If you hear good news, believe it. If you hear bad news – wait a little while till it is confirmed but I cannot think any, but glorious tidings will be returned from us.

Keep a good heart.

I was much surprised and pleased to see the letter from mother to Palin. She writes so sprightly that it did me good. Be economical with the "needful." I need not tell you that but do not stint yourselves. Kiss all the little ones for me. Remember me to Emily [Sam's sister] and Mr. Smith [Albert Smith, Emily's husband] and the children. Also to Mssrs. Bloor. They have written me that business is very dull. They must write to me after you tell them. Henry B. owes me a letter.

> I remain in Hope
> Your affectionate Brother,
> Samuel

. . . Charley [Sam's younger brother] must remember me to his wife.

ON BOARD GUNBOAT LANCER
JANUARY 8, 1862

Dear Sister,

We left our camp on Monday morning and got safely on board the propeller "Lancer." Pretty much all the troops are now embarked. Our regiment is divided between this boat and the gunboat "Pioneer."

There are some thirty boats in the bay around us and we expect to leave for Fort Monroe at 12 [o'clock].

You will direct your letters thus (Capt. S.H. Sims, Co. G, 51st Regt. N.Y. Vols. on board Gunboat Lancer). You might add "Genl. Burnside's expedition."

I have a berth in the cabin and we are very comfortable. Palin is on board of the "Pioneer." This boat although it mounts four guns is not intended for more than a "transport" ship and will not likely go before any [artillery] batteries.

The men are all "bunked" pretty close, and at first there was a good deal of confusion, but now every thing is in good order.

No matter if you are uncertain about letters reaching me, send a line by every opportunity.

Remember me all at home and take the "[New York] Times" and "[Brooklyn] Eagle" everyday and let Sammy read the news. I will write from "Fortress Monroe" where it is likely we shall lay some time. We shall be almost within sight of Norfolk and the Rebel batteries there. Sammy can see the place on the map.

We have perfect health and are all in first rate spirits. Breakfast is ready and I will close.

Your affectionate Brother
Samuel

On Board Gunboat Lancer
January 10, 1862

Dear Sister,

We have just cast anchor off "Fortress Monroe" it is nearly nine o'clock. Our passage down the Chesapeake Bay was delayed by a heavy fog which lasted twelve hours and obliged us to anchor.

Everything has thus far passed off pleasantly. All our men are in good health and eager to see the enemy. How soon that may be I cannot tell. We may lay here some time before the final start.

Your letter may now be addressed to this place. It is a beautiful sight to see the large number of war ships congregated here with their numerous lights.

We have on board our boat the reporter of the "New York Times." His name is Aug. Rawlings. Mr. Bloor is acquainted with his father and so am I for he owes our firm over four hundred dollars and I suppose he always will. The reporter is a jolly fellow and we have jolly times with him. You will no doubt read his letters in the "Times."

Our boat is the fastest of the fleet that started from Annapolis and we gained on all the rest until the fog came on. The "breaking up" of our camp before the start was a sight but seldom witnessed. The tents were struck long before daylight, and the fires lighted in the camps about, lit up the country around for miles. Most every tent had its evergreen trees about them and all of these were set on fire. The ground was covered with snow and reflected the light almost brighter than day.

The weather is now very mild and with the moon shining bright, it is quite pleasant on deck.

Commodore (later Rear Admiral) Silas Stringham (1798-1876), who served as flag officer of the Atlantic Blockade Squadron early in the Civil War. He is interred at Green-Wood Cemetery. Courtesy of the Library of Congress.

You see that I have no particular news to give you. I would like to write a long letter but cannot find anything interesting and do not care about romancing for I would make but a poor hand at it.

I am in first rate health. Palin is on board of the "Pioneer." The Lieut. Col. of our regiment is in command there. He told our colonel that he thought a good deal of Sergeant [Palin] Sims.

I often imagine myself home in the kitchen. I can see it, and every part of it. That spot in the window where Ellie tore the paper looks bad. You can find some of the same kind of paper in the closet under the stairs. That carpet on the floor looks very shabby and I am afraid Henry will trip up and fall on the stove. I see that Charlie [Sam's younger brother] has not trimmed the grape vine yet. This should be done before the month of March. If I had time I would try the handle of the pump to see if the cistern has been cemented yet. Sammy must shovel off the snow and not let it freeze on the front door so much. So you must get a new carpet and have the cistern fixed and Charlie must trim the vine. I have got as much as I can attend to for some little time to come and the home guard must stir about.

I will write soon again. Do not fail to write.

Your Bro[ther], Samuel

ON BOARD GUNBOAT LANCER
HATTERAS INLET – COAST OF NORTH CAROLINA
JANUARY 14TH 1862

Dear Sister,

We arrived at this place yesterday after a pretty rough passage. Most of the fleet arrived before us on account of our captain taking a course further out to sea than the rest. The vessels with the "left wing" of our regiment, were here before us. The weather is very bad, and the vessels although lying near to each other, cannot communicate together. I have not seen Palin since we left Fortress Monroe.

A few minutes before leaving Fort Monroe I enclosed a few lines to you, which were from Palin, and intended for Mother.

This place is where the rebels had a chance to send out their "privateers" until the expedition of General [Benjamin] Butler and Commodore [Silas] Stringham took possession of the fort, which lays about six hundred yards from our vessels. The fort is built of sand and earth and shows the marks of the balls on it. A more desolate place than the sandy flats you could not imagine. The winds have full sweep and there are no hills for shelter. The weather is so rough that we have been delayed from proceeding up the Pamlico Sound which appears to be the scene for our operation.

One vessel, an upended gunboat now lays a wreck in full sight from our ship and there is no chance of assisting her. Her masts have been cut away one by one, and they have just thrown overboard her smoke pipe. The sea beats completely over her and if the weather continues so bad, she will be a total loss.

On our passage out, most of the officers were sick. I was not affected in the least, and had a good time assisting about the ship. At one time it was thought we should have to put back, but our colonel would not hear of it. We "laid to" some six hours until daylight, and then steamed for the inlet and finally got in all safe.

The delay which we are experiencing will give the rebels a chance to fortify the different points on the sound, and the numerous creeks and inlets, for I suppose the news of our arrival has been spread throughout the country about. It appears to have been the intention of Genl. Burnside, for the different regiments to separate in different directions and occupy positions in the country. The counties bordering on the sea have been represented as being strong for the Union and I suppose it is hoped that the resistance to the troops will be but little. However, I suppose that no loyalty will be developed until our strength is proven.

As soon as the weather moderates, no doubt we shall move on. I have seen no sign of quailing among either our officers or men. No doubt all will fight well. The colonel [Edward Ferrero] has grown deeper into the esteem and confidence of the regiment. He is cool and determined.

In our cabin we have twenty-four berths occupied by the officers. The colonel is with us and is the life of the party. When the storm was at its height and everything moveable was rattling back and forth, the dishes smashing, the colonel had his jokes ready and under the circumstances everything went off quite pleasantly, although the pitching of the vessel was fearful. I was on deck most of the time.

The cape is considered one of the most stormy places on the whole coast, and I believe it. Several wrecks are in the neighborhood of our anchorage. We can but just see the mainland. On the map Sammy can find "Cape Hatteras" and a few miles below the inlet in which we lay. The town of "Newbern" I believe will be one of our points of attack, also the other towns on the rivers emptying into the "Pamlico Sound."

While we lay at Fortress Monroe the rebel camp at Craney Island was in sight and we could see the flash of their guns practicing at the target. It was reported that a vessel came out from Norfolk and took note of each vessel as it arrived at Fort Monroe. I hope the information will do them good. I saw a large number of "contrabands" outside at "Old Point Comfort." The men are employed in carting provisions and supplies for the army.

The government in fitting up vessels for our expedition has taken several of the ferry boats from the Brooklyn and Jersey City ferries and they look quite saucy with the rail all plated with iron sheets and holes pierced for muskets. The platforms where carriages and carts used to stand are now occupied by large flat boats for landing troops. There are also the material for making "pontoon bridges."

It is now 9 ½ o'clock p.m. and the weather looks stormy yet. I will quit writing for tonight and "turn in."

Pencil sketch by Captain Sims, 1864: "Escape of 'contrabands' from Colonel Avery's estate near Petersburg, Virginia." It is signed at left, "S.H.S.," for Samuel Harris Sims. The Avery estate house was used by Union forces as an observation post; it was also used by Major General Gouverneur Kemble Warren, while in command of the Fifth Corps, Army of the Potomac, as his headquarters.

[LETTER CONTINUES] WEDNESDAY MORNING, JAN 15TH

I have just heard from Palin's ship. They got along very well. The vessel I spoke of last night has gone to pieces as near as we can make out.

The weather has moderated a good deal.

The chaplain is going ashore after breakfast and will take all the letters so I must close by wishing that all will go well with us and that we shall meet with success I do not doubt. So farewell for the present.

From your affectionate
Samuel

ON BOARD GUNBOAT LANCER
PAMLICO SOUNDS
JANUARY 28, 1862

Dear Sister,

I take the advantage of a vessel leaving here tomorrow to send you a line.

Not knowing whether or not you have received any of my letters since we left Fortress Monroe I will state that we got here at Hatteras Inlet (after a pretty rough passage) on the thirteenth of Jan. Since that date we have been laying off the Fort, and eating the government rations.

We had no idea that we should be so long lying idle. The last three days have been favorable and the vessel has had her stores replenished from the provision ships.

A more stormy place you could not conceive. The ship rolls almost constantly and we have got what the sailors call "our sea legs on", that means that we can walk the decks without falling. But I am afraid that we shall all get bandy legged and roll about when we get ashore which will look clumsy but may be of advantage in dodging the "secesh" shots.

I hardly think you would know me, for I have got so fat. My coat will hardly meet and I have got cheeks on. Our fare is pretty hard at times. Hard bread at times with a dab of molasses has been our supper. But as a general thing there has been but little complaint. Yesterday a party from our ship went up the sound and stopped a boat and took from it some fresh shad! We had it for our supper. Our major also went ashore and shot some ducks and also three sheep which appeared to be wild. They were quite small.

Whenever the sea is any way smooth small parties go out visiting the different vessels of the expedition. There are somewhere near one hundred and thirty vessels of different kinds belonging to the expedition. Quite a number have been lost.

The second Lieutenant of my company arrived here today. He was detached from my company at Annapolis, to serve in the Signal Corps, and left after us on board a schooner. A report came to us the other day of a number of soldiers having been washed ashore about five miles up the coast and we were almost certain that it was the men belonging to the Signal Corp schooner. But we were much relieved when Lieutenant [William H.] Barker's arrival proved the contrary. The poor fellow has had a hard time [he got typhoid fever – but would live until 1924]. They were driven far out to sea and had a miserable time of it. He is begging hard to be permitted to rejoin his company.

I have seen New York papers dated Jan. 22nd. They contain surmises of our intended operations, which may prove true. Some of them say "we have no doubt but the blow is struck by this time." There are a good many points on the "inland coast" where the rebels might expect us. And I think that we shall be able to "make up" for our long delay by taking some of them by surprise yet. We may possibly push on in a day or two (it is quite uncertain) and our destination may be "Roanoke Island" which lays some sixty miles north of us.

The heavy draught of many of the vessels has delayed our expedition very much; and it is as much as we could do to get over the "Bar", and into deep water. We were literally (sic) dragged over the sand and I thought at one time that we would bump the bottom out of the vessel; but we got through safe and sound and are ready for duty.

Our men are in good health and spirits. Very little sickness on board. One man died three days ago and was buried in the sand on shore. I have seen no frost since we left Annapolis. The men have bathed on the shore not finding it too cold. Our evenings are spent in choir singing and reading and writing. The Col. is full of fun and we have lively times in the cabin.

Water is scarce and we have to deal it out by measure. The Colonel [Ferrero] has placed me in charge of the water department. I would give anything for that Powers St. pump [in Bushwick, Brooklyn] or the faucet in Emily's bath room. The water we drink now is made from sea water purified from salt by passing through boilers and the steam condensed. We are getting used to it but high prices would be paid for supplies of clear Croton or Ridgewood [two New York drinking waters].

Now you must not write less than two letters per week and you must send them by every extra opportunity which offers, such as vessels leaving direct for the expedition. I am as anxious to hear from you as you are to hear from me. Palin is well and mother must write to him for he talks a good deal about you all when I visit his ship. Palin may possibly come on board our ship to stay. I shall try to have him.

You will direct your letters to Capt. S. H. Sims, Co. G, 51st Regiment New York vols., Genl Burnside's expedition. Make the directions plain as there is a 51st Pennsylvania regiment and sometimes our letters get mixed. I wrote to Emily [Sam's sister] and soon expect an answer.

I hope the next letter you get from me will contain something more interesting than this. Something that will be worth writing about. Something that will be history.

I can seldom find good opportunities to write, so you must let this go around for all who are interested. With prayers for your comfort at home I will close. Kiss the children for me. Try to send their photograph, also your own and mothers, and if Em would send hers it would delight me. Try to do this. God bless you and keep you all until peace comes and allows us to return home.

> Your affectionate brother,
> Sam

This is the Battle Song of the 51st Regiment, "as sung by them when approaching the enemy on the shores of North Carolina February 5, 1862." It was written by Chaplain Orlando N. Ben-

The first page of the 51st's handwritten battle song, written by its chaplain, Orlando N. Benton. The Green-Wood Historic Fund Collections.

ton, age 34 years, of the 51st, who would be mortally wounded at the next battle the 51st fought, at Newbern, North Carolina, on March 14, 1862; he died the next day. The Battle Song was dedicated to the 51st's colonel, Edward Ferrero. The "Jeff" referred to in the lyrics below is Jefferson Davis, Confederate president.

Say Rebels will you meet us?
Say Rebels will you greet us!
Say Rebels will you beat us.
On North Carolina's shores

In the name of God we meet you,
With the sword of God we greet you,
By the grace of God we beat you.
On North Carolina's shore.

Singing Glory Hallelujah!
Singing Glory Hallelujah!
Singing Glory Hallelujah!
To God forever more.

In the name of Jeff you meet us.
With the sword of Jeff you greet us;
In treason's name to beat us.
On North Carolina's shore.

But our flag shall float forever
And our Union none shall sever;
And freedom perish never
On North Carolina's shore,

Oh, then glory Hallelujah
Oh, then glory Hallelujah
Oh, then glory Hallelujah
To God forevermore!

The Battle of Roanoke, anticipated for weeks – Captain Sims and his comrades had been on transport ships for a month before it was fought – took place on February 8, 1862. This was the first phase of

Roanoke

Brigadier General Ambrose Burnside's planned North Carolina Expedition. Union forces at Roanoke comprised three brigades totaling 14 regiments, supported by eight Army gunboats and twenty Navy ships. The Confederates under Brigadier General Henry Wise countered with six regiments and eight ships of the Confederate Navy.

On February 7, Burnside landed 7,500 soldiers on Roanoke Island. The next day, the Union forces moved against the Confederate forts and their outnumbered defenders. After suffering fewer than 100 casualties, Confederate Colonel H.M. Shaw surrendered 2,500 soldiers and 32 artillery pieces. Union forces now held an important outpost on the Atlantic – one that they would hold through the rest of the war.

The 51st was heavily engaged during the Battle of Roanoke, the first time it had "seen the elephant," and suffered 23 casualties: 3 killed, 11 wounded, and 9 missing. Colonel Edward Ferrero, commanding the 51st, cited Captain Sims in his field report for taking possession of the guns at the enemy fort after the Confederates retreated. Ferrero also reported: "The men and officers under my command behaved with a coolness that was really surprising for men who were under fire for their first time."

On February 12, 1862, the _New York Times_ published two accounts of Burnside's Expedition – apparently written by August Rawlings, to whom Sims referred by name in his January 5 letter. Captains Sims was mentioned in one of those published reports.

BURNSIDE EXPEDITION
ROANOKE ISLAND
MARCH 4, 1862

Dear Sister,

I received yours, Sammy, and Lucy's of the 13th February. We are just about to re-embark on board the transports again for another expedition.

You will hear of us before this reaches you, as usual our destination is unknown to us.

I have full hope that we shall succeed again. We may possibly have it pretty rough but hopes are entertained, and expressed, by our Generals that we shall gain a point that will go far towards ending this war.

We are both, Palin and I, in good health. I have heard that our letters have been delayed at Hatteras Inlet. The communication with the North is irregular.

I have seen New York papers to 21st February (Tribune). I have no word in any of your letters of how Charlie is nor Mr. Bloor. I have seen accounts that the Hawkins Zouaves [the 9th New York Infantry, which took part in the attack at Roanoke Island] were the first to charge the battery here. It was not so. But it makes little difference.

Last evening we received Em's letter and one from Mary Lib and one huge one from Willy.

[The water] is good enough to drink with the eyes shut . . . We are used to it.

We eat ducks (wild) and have lots of shad (12 cents for 6 pounders). We have eggs too in abundance. We pay 5 cents a piece for apples – 50 cents a pound for raisins – 50 cents for cheese. These things are all from the Sutler who brings them from the north. Sutlers make lots of money.

Some of our wounded men are going home soon. My wounded are all recovering fast. I have not lost a man since we left N.Y. Most of the companies have suffered severely in losing men. There has been six of A Company (quartered near me) buried in the last two weeks from fevers. Our men go in bathing here while Sammy is skating in Brooklyn. The buds in the bushes are swelling and planting season will soon set in.

A good many Contrabands [ex-slaves] come to the Island having escaped from different points on the Sound.

We had a celebration in our Camps on hearing of [the Union victories at] Forts Henry and Donelson [in Tennessee]. We have also [heard] that Memphis, Savannah, and Nashville have been surrendered to us. All here are in the best of spirits.

Recollect Lucretia that the next thing pleasant to hearing of victories is the arrival of a mail with letters for us. Direct to me as usual. Letters will be forwarded to us. This must do for all as the opportunity of writing is scarce just now and the mail is so uncertain. I understand that this will leave the Island today. I trust that we next may go by way of Norfolk. We shall see.

We may soon be home in Brooklyn. No more at present.

God bless you all,
Sam

Newbern, North Carolina was strategically located at the confluence of the Trent and Neuse Rivers, near the Atlantic coast. The Atlantic and North Carolina Railroad ran through Newbern. The 51st fought there, again as a part of Burnside's Expedition, on March 14. As at Roanoke Island, the Union forces outnumbered the Confederates and were supported by substantial Naval forces. The Federals broke the Confederate line and captured Newbern, holding it through the rest of the war. But casualties for the 51st at Newbern were heavy: 3 officers and 31 enlisted men were killed, and 4 officers and 37 enlisted men were wounded.

"Camp Newbern"
Near Newbern City, North Carolina
March 21, 1862

Dear Henry [Bloor],
The "Times" came to hand the second day after the Battle. I have been waiting patiently to hear a word from you.

We are quartered in the late Rebel Barracks, a stones throw from the Neuse River, and 2 ½ miles from the Battle field.

Along the shore south-east of us there are five Batteries heavily mounted and most formidable. But the right flag floats over them now.

Our victory here was preceded (as at Roanoke) by a night of exposure in the rain, without shelter. The events of the next day proved that the ardor of our men had not been dampened with their clothes;

and also that our <u>powder</u> was kept dry. They say we fought nearly four hours. Time runs queer when you are under fire. My boys fired their 60 rounds [each soldier went into battle with 60 cartridges for his musket], and as much more as we could get from the dead and wounded before we could drive those rascals from their den.

It looked a little blue at one time when our ammunition was giving out. No wonder that the rebel fire was so incessant, they had double our numbers behind that "breastwork" [a temporary

"The Battle of New Bern." *Harper's Weekly*, April 5, 1862.

fortification, usually of wood or earth to breast height, protecting soldiers as they stood and fired] and re-enforcements coming in. General [Jesse] Reno is with us, and has ordered us to "fall back" and let the "51st Penn" take our place, my boys say, they, "be d-d if they do." And they <u>did</u> not, for at that instant a white flag <u>saw we</u> and we were in that Battery double quick.

Seven of my boys were wounded. One in the breast. One had his right arm shattered. One lost a thumb, one a little finger, one was struck in the cheek and the ball lodged in the roof of his mouth. Another was struck by a ball near the thigh. Several had their rifles struck from their hands. Two had balls pass through their caps.

Out of 24 of our officers 3 were killed and 3 wounded. Our Lieutenant Colonel [Robert Brown] Potter was struck by my side. The chaplain [Reverend Orlando N. Benton] was behind us when he was shot. Capt. David R. Johnson and his Lieutenant [George D.] Allen were killed to my left. Lieutenant [Abraham W.] McKee was shot through the leg. Another Lieutenant [Francis W. Tryon] was shot through the thigh. Major [Charles William] LeGendre has a terrible wound in his face. All of these officers were dressed in thick dark blue uniforms, and were, no doubt singled out. I had a light Blue overcoat, and appeared as the men but I did not escape the attentions of the cowardly foe [sharpshooters].

General Burnside says that "we had the "key" of the position." I should think so too, it seemed like a dead lock there. Oh! How cool my men were, veterans could not do better.

I did not see one sign of fear in all that terrible fire. Imagine how thick the shots flew! A tree about three inches in diameter, which stood in front of our position, shows the marks of 14 shots, from the ground, up as high as you could reach; we were protected by a slight rise in the ground and a few trees against which the thud thud thud was incessant. Birds were picked up that had been killed in their flight between the fires.

Talk of "chivalry" now. To see those gentry run from their works in terror; made me ashamed that they had been Americans and citizens of the United States. I don't believe they have stopped running yet. Some of them were drowned four miles away while trying to ford a creek! They left their arms (loaded) all the way for miles in every direction. We have taken an immense quantity of cannon and ammunition. It is surprising how many Union men you find among these scarecrows who fought us. If I was a rebel I would stick to it.

After we had buried our dead and looked to the comforts of our wounded, I started with some officers through the country. I would like to give you an account of this trip for I think you would be interested very much. We passed the night on a cotton plantation, and I slept there very uncomfortably on a feather bed belonging to a wealthy planter. Truly, a soldier's life has "ups and downs."

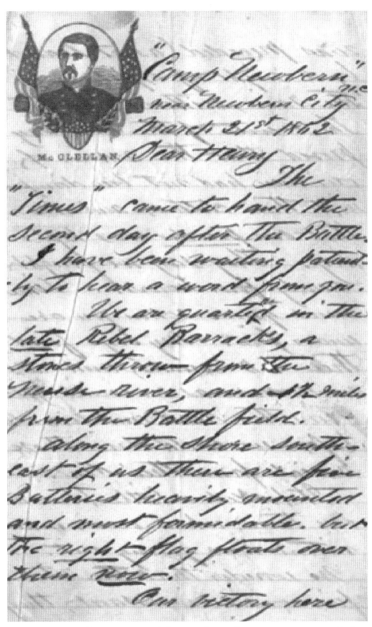

The first page of Captain Sims's letter of March 21, 1862. At upper left is the image of Major General George B. McClellan; when this letter was written, McClellan was in command of the Union's Army of the Potomac. The Green-Wood Historic Fund Collections.

The people are returning to their homes about here and are surprised at the kind treatment they receive. I have enclosed some
specimen of the letters found about here in a box of "notions", sent
home to my sister.

Our regiment has suffered so severely that it is likely we shall
have to remain some time to recruit. I have lots of trophies and
would like to send you some if there was a way to do so. I have <u>my</u>
horse to ride, and I <u>had</u> a sail <u>boat,</u> but some scamp or another has
stolen it. ("<u>Won</u> <u>it</u>" – is the term <u>we</u> use.)

There has been <u>talk</u> of <u>retaking</u> this place. Jefferson Davis [the
president of the Confederacy], in order to do that, will have to
meet us on a <u>fair</u> field. I do not think he dares to do it.

Three of our men were taken prisoners by their cavalry a few
miles out of this city. It is said there are 1200 cavalry hovering
about, etc. etc.

Now <u>do</u> write me a letter I "want to know" how you are getting along very much. Will you give my kind remembrances to Mrs.
Bloor and her mother, sisters, & brother. Also to William and his
wife and to your sister.

Mr. Knott has sent his regards to myself, through a letter from
the father of one of my men, that I had to leave on Roanoke; ([Ser-
geant] Fred McReady) a brave man as ever lived and who cried
bitterly because he could not come with me.)

I have been specially favored in my command. I have not lost a
man by death since we left N. York. The other companies have all
suffered in losing men by sickness and killed in action.

Colonel [Edward] Ferrero has notified me that my company is
to be first to go on picket. Thus it is. First to land on Roanoke. First
company as skirmishers there. First to stand guard on that Island.
First in the Battery there. Now we are to be the first to establish
picket duty beyond our lines. So as the war ends soon I am satisfied
to do, for I cannot help myself.

Hoping this will find you all well.

I remain truly yours

Sam

Drummer Jesse W. Mills had enlisted as a teenager, early in the Civil War, to serve in the 13th Regiment, Company B, under then-Lieutenant Samuel Sims. At the time of his enlistment, Mills had gray eyes, black hair, a fair complexion, and was 5' 7".

After Sims was discharged from the 13th and turned his energies towards recruiting Company G of the 51st, young Jesse re-enlisted and served as the drummer of that company until the war was over and he was discharged on July 25, 1865.

At the Battle of Newbern, Mills had bravely drummed the 51st into battle; for his unflinching courage, a ceremony was held at Camp Potter near Newbern on June 9, 1862, in which Captain Sims called out his company to witness his presentation to Mills of two sets of drum sticks. One set was capped with silver mounts and inscribed: "To/Jesse Mills/from/Company B 13th Regt./N.Y.S.M." – Sims's and Mills's company in the old 13th. As per a newspaper account of this ceremony, "In making the presentation Captain Sims had the company drawn up in front of his quarters and addressed his men in a very appropriate manner, remarking that these gifts were evidence that they were not forgotten at home; he was much pleased to present these testimonials of the kind regard of their friends." Captain Sims told his men that he was particularly happy to give these drumsticks to Jesse "as he had always performed his duty and was ever a reliable man in his company." The account concludes: "The Captain then proposed three hearty cheers for Company B of the 13th Regiment of Brooklyn, which were heartily given as only Company G can give them."

CAMP POTTER NEAR NEWBERN, NORTH CAROLINA
JUNE 14, 1862

Dear Henry [Bloor],
  . . . We are located about four miles from the city of Newbern on the banks of the Kent River. This is <u>nothing</u> doing in the shape of

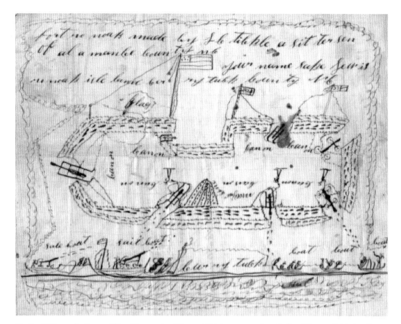

Rebel Sketch found by Captain Sims. Written on back by Sims: "Picked up at the Battery on the Coast give this to H. Bloor with my compliments ask him to read it if he can and give me an interpretation. It is a plan of one of the coast Batteries which is now in our possession." The Green-Wood Historic Fund Collections.

"movements", with occasionally a little scouting party of a company or tow in the neighborhood of the skedaddling rebel pickets. We have nothing but the usual routine of camp life. The divisions however have promises of something to do and we keep awake in anticipation.

The woods and rivers here furnish us plenty of amusement in shape of game. William would be delighted in this country. The snakes invade our tents at night. Some very large of the moccasin variety and others too numerous to mention. All kinds of birds too abound. The mocking birds are very plenty. . . .

The city of Newbern has been and is now quite a California to speculators in goods required by the men of our division. The scarcity of white men outside of those attached to the army has given the darkies a chance which they have improved, and they have salted down all the specie which was brought by the troops. A great many men from the north are laying in stocks of goods in anticipation of peace being soon made and the country opened for trade.

We are blowing up the rebel forts in the Neuse River with their own powder. I witnessed the destruction of one yesterday, the sight was very fine. Our line of defense for our position is now completed and is a splendid work. We shall not require them we hope.

A mail today brings us intelligence of our gunboats being near to Charleston, South Carolina. We feel a little disappointed for it was our wish to go to that infernal pest hole. However we have all North Carolina before us, and there is a division of Rebel troops at Kingston and another at Goldsboro if they will wait a little while I think General Burnside will give us permission to visit them by the rail-road line to those places.

We are in splendid condition and pretty well acquainted. This is considered an unhealthy country but our men although exposed to malaria from swamps and fatigue duty at night are har-

Drummer Jesse Mills, who served loyally with Captain Sims during the Civil War.

The 9th Corps was formed on July 22, 1862, with Major General Ambrose Burnside in command. Captain Sims, a skilled artist, designed the 9th Corps badge. The Green-Wood Historic Fund Collections.

dy and well. Our regimental sick list shows an average of but 2 men complaining with slight disorders of the bowels. It is pretty warm and I fear you will find this a dull letter. So I will close trusting it may find you all in good health and business improving. Please remember me to Mrs. Bloor and to Mr. & Mrs. William V. Bloor.

In hopes of hearing again from 364 [Atlantic Avenue, where Henry P. Bloor and his brother William V. Bloor worked as glass stainers – and where Sam had worked for them] I will wind up.

> Truly yours
> Sam

The 51st Regiment remained quartered at Newbern until July 6, 1862. It was then ordered to return from North Carolina to Virginia, and arrived at Newport News to join Major General John Pope's campaign with the Army of Virginia from August 21 through September 2.

[ABOARD SHIP] CHESAPEAKE
AUGUST 3, 1862

Dear Sister [Lucretia],

We are on the way with Burnside's Division, to Aquia Creek, Virginia sixty miles below Washington. I suppose we are to co-operate with General [John] Pope.

I am much surprised at my not hearing from you and especially as I wrote particularly ten days ago for information.

Palin came up from Newbern on Thursday. He is quite fat but is troubled a little with the piles. He is with us on board.

It is likely we will be paid in a few days but I feel discouraged about sending money forward on account of my not hearing from you and the fact that I do not know whether you have received the forty dollars I sent from Newbern one month ago. I also feel anxious to know whether Mr. Read called on you.

Our men are all in good condition, scarcely a sick man in the regiment. We shall most likely be in a country more healthy when we get to our destination and with the chances of foraging we will be able to live handsomely.

I beg of you not to fail to write to me directly. Our division is now termed the "9th Army Corps" address your envelope - You might get Mr. Bloor to address the letter.

Capt. Saml. H. Sims
Co. G 51st Regt N.Y.V.
"Burnside Division"
9th Army Corps
Fredericksburg, VA (or elsewhere)

We are anxious to fill up our regiment with new recruits. The plan of raising new regiments is condemned by all of us here. Fill up the old army to the standard again and there will be troops enough to clear a way in any direction south. [For political reasons, new recruits by and large were assigned to new regiments – so that officer commissions for those new regiments could be awarded to those in favor with the various state governors].

I wrote to Mr. William V. Bloor at the same time I posted a letter to you. Probably I shall meet his brother-in-law in the 14th Brooklyn [officially designated the 84th New York Infantry] if they are at Fredericksburg.

I hear it said that we may stop at camp at Aquia Creek to await any call for us again on the coast – or to assist [Major General George] McClellan. It is also said that McClellan will bring his army back to start again on his original plan [McClellan had just failed spectacularly in his efforts to lead the Army of the Potomac up the Virginia peninsula to capture the Confederate capital,

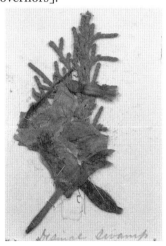

These flowers, picked by Captain Sims in Virginia's Dismal Swamp during his service, were sent to his fiancée, Carrie Dayton. The Green-Wood Historic Fund Collections.

Richmond]. We shall soon become "Marines" if we have many more sea trips. Truly we are a shifting division. Now here, now there.

Palin was saying that Charlie [Sam's youngest brother] might take a notion to come out. He must not think of it for he could not stand the service. Typhoid fever surely seizes those who are inclined to be bilious – and as Charlie has had so many attacks of fever it would be the utmost folly for him to join the army. There is enough of Simses in the field at present so if he has had any notion of the kind it is best to dismiss it. [Just weeks later, on August 20, 1862, Charles Sims enlisted in the 48th New York Volunteer Infantry.]

[LETTER CONTINUES] NEAR FREDERICKSBURG, VIRGINIA
AUGUST 5, 1862 TUESDAY MORNING

We arrived at this place last night and bivouacked on the ground. We are about to pitch our tents. It is a beautiful hilly country around the city, from which we are about 3 miles distant. I heard last night that the 14th Brooklyn are about to start on a scout. There is nothing more today than that you must write.

> From your affectionate brother,
> Sam

In August, the 51st joined Major General John Pope's campaign in Virginia. It fought at Kelly's Ford, Sulphur Springs, Second Bull Run, and Chantilly. The 51st suffered 89 casualties at these battles, including 23 enlisted men killed. The regiment then was withdrawn to Washington, D.C., but after only two days it was back in the field for the Maryland Campaign, marching north with the Army of the Potomac under Major General George McClellan. The 51st took 16 casualties at South Mountain and 87 killed or wounded at Antietam, the bloodiest single day in American history. There the 51st fought its way, along with the 51st Pennsylvania Infantry, across what would become known as Burnside's Bridge in "a most brilliant charge across the stone bridge, which alone would have made the fighting qualities of the regiment renowned."

Dear Sister,

The slip I enclose could not be sent; correspondence being temporarily cut off at the time. After dark last evening we marched with our division "Reno's" from Alexandria and arrived in Washington much fatigued, at 3 o'clock this (Friday) morning. From what I can learn we shall gain a little time here for much needed repose. It is said we shall garrison Washington under Burnside, but there is no telling. A large mail reached here for our men. It has been gathering over a month.

Our regiment has passed through most of the fighting with [Confederate General Stonewall] Jackson's and [Confederate General Robert E.] Lee's commands. We were supporting [artillery] batteries [specifically Durell's Battery, also referred to as Independent Battery D, Pennsylvania Volunteer Artillery] and a good part of the fighting at [the Battle of Second] Bull Run passed directly before us. We were exposed constantly to fire from shells and missiles but have escaped with a loss in killed and wounded of about sixty and there is probably thirty missing men.

I know how anxious you must have been when this news of the fighting was first published but I believe you have strength of mind sufficient to bear up under the infliction and suspense which is worst of all.

The scenes I have witnessed I cannot write but I will say that however it may appear to you in the North – our men have behaved nobly in every code. I speak from observation, for the whole battlefield was spread out before us and every movement was discernable by us. The failure to drive the rebels is accounted for by several of us. It is not proper though for me to speak of them. Others will attend to the fault I sincerely hope.

The 14th Brooklyn were terribly cut up. They rallied near our lines with but a handful of men bearing their colors with them. Two of their officers I helped to carry were badly wounded. I know most all of their officers for we were once together in one company under [Rhode Island Governor William] Sprague. I can not help saying that their almost total extermination is the fruit of a deliberate plan laid by a <u>traitor</u>, who sent them to certain defeat well knowing it before hand. [This may be a veiled reference to Major General Irvin McDowell, who commanded the Third Corps at Second Bull Run, which included the 14th Brooklyn, and also was labeled a "traitor" by others]. Enough of this, but it is the talk of us all.

I will give you a list of my wounded who were left on the field and of course fell into the hands of our enemy. They are probably now in this city or Alexandria as all the wounded have been paroled and released.

> John Martin
> Joseph Megee
> James McGinnis
> Jos. P. Nagle (slightly)
> Jas. McCormick
> Corpl. Robt. Wethered

None of them are seriously wounded that I know of.

Palin is safe. He has been with the ammunition wagon all the time. He has gone to the city this morning to see the folks.

I must close with thanks to God for our safety and good health through all the perils of the last three weeks.

My hope is strong that better days for the cause are close at hand and our apparent reverses are soon proved to be victorious. This I pray.

> With love to you all,
> Sam

BANKS OF MONOCACY CREEK
NEAR FREDERICK CITY, MARYLAND
SEPTEMBER 13, 1862

Dear Sister [Lucretia],

To relieve your wondering as to where we are I take a chance to send a line.

We left Alexandria on the 4th of this month and arrived in Washington over the Long Bridge next morning. We stayed two days in Washington and then marched north through Maryland stopping to bivouac at night only.

We have had but little rest. We now have marching orders and it may be that this letter may miss being posted.

I am in good health and stand the marching well. Several of our officers have broken down with fatigue, but, I am thankful to say such has not been my case.

As I write I hear the roar of artillery beyond the City of Frederick [Maryland]. An artillery duel is going on between our batteries (3 I hear) and two of the rebels. We have chased a division of rebels through a section of Maryland and hope to soon bring them to a stand.

I hear but little news of the general movements of the army. We are now under [Major General Ambrose] Burnside in the division of General [Jesse] Reno and again under the immediate command of General [Samuel] Sturgis. The rebs have evacuated Frederick City. They passed through Maryland I think for the last time. It is a beautiful country through which we have passed and the people seem to be good Union people.

I have hard times to satisfy my English notions of "grub." However I manage to get along with the aid of my boy Jack [likely a recently-freed slave] who is smart in foraging. I make my pot of mush and it goes good. Hard bread has become quite tasty. We get a good many apples along the roads. When we stop occasionally I find some little house where I get a supper or dinner, such as it is.

I am full of hope as to the speedy finishing of the war. The people in Maryland here have been robbed of a good deal of property (horses and cattle, provisions, etc.) by the Rebels as they passed through.

Virginia is quite exhausted. There is such a difference between the look of the two states that the horrors of war are more apparent and more to be dreaded. How I pray for peace and how thankful I am to have every reason to hope that you are comfortable at home.

My company is now quite large. A number of recruits have

"The Charge Across Burnside Bridge, Antietam, 1 PM Sept. 17, 1862," by Edwin Forbes. Forbes was one of the leading sketch artists of the Civil War; he is interred at Green-Wood. Private Thomas Stockwell and many other brave Union men died in the repeated assaults across this bridge, cut down by Confederates who had an open line of fire from a hill on the opposite side of Antietam Creek and concentrated targets in blue.

joined us and to a man they wish to join my company. Their wishes are considered by the Colonel and they are placed in my charge.

I have heard nothing of my wounded men at "Bull Run" or "Chantilly." I think they must be either in [hospitals in] Washington or Alexandria. I wrote you from Washington directing you to see Mr. Nagle about his son who was wounded slightly at Bull Run. Have you seen him?

I will close for fear of missing the mail. Palin is well.

With love to all, I am
Sam

Thomas Stockwell, according to the 1860 United States census, worked as a paperhanger and owned personal property totaling $200. He lived with his wife, Caroline, and their three children, Henry, Frances, and Edward, ages 11, 8, and 2, respectively, at 279 Myrtle Avenue in Brooklyn. On September 4, 1861, he enlisted in the 51st New York Volunteer Infantry as a private and mustered into Company G – Captain Sims's – eight days later. A year later, on September 17, 1862, Stockwell was killed at Burnside's Bridge as he, his comrades in the 51st, and the men of the 51st Pennsylvania Infantry, repeatedly attempted to cross a bridge over Antietam Creek under heavy Confederate fire from a hill beyond the bridge. His comrades interred him on the battlefield, at the base of the bridge that he had died trying to cross. Two months after his death, his widow was granted a pension by the federal government. In the spring of 1863, Stockwell's body was dug from its battlefield grave by undertaker William B. Van Brunt of Brooklyn, who brought it back to Brooklyn. Private Thomas Stockwell was interred in grave 69 in the Civil War Soldiers' Lot at Green-Wood Cemetery on April 11, 1863.

Photograph taken at the base of Burnside's Bridge, where Union troops, killed at the Battle of Antietam attempting to cross what would be known from that day forward as Burnside's Bridge, were temporarily interred. The wooden boards at the base of the stone wall were carved as temporary gravestones to identify the dead. Though it is impossible to read all of these inscriptions, one of these boards likely marked the grave of Private Thomas Stockwell. The bridge is in the background. The photograph dates from just a few days after the battle. Courtesy of the Library of Congress.

HEADQUARTERS, 51ST REGIMENT NEW YORK VOLUNTEERS
NEAR VILLAGE OF ANTIETAM MARYLAND
SEPT 22, 1862

Mrs. Thomas Stockwell

Dear Madame,

It has become my most painful and unavoidable duty to announce to you the death of your husband. He was killed while in the faithful discharge of his duty at the storming of Antietam Bridge Maryland in the morning of September 17th 1862. Our joy at gaining the victory that day has been restrained by our remembrance of the brave men who fell – the faces of our comrades once so familiar that are lost to us, and more than that, the grief that we know will be brought to the home of our noble brother who has rendered his life a sacrifice to prove his devotion to our country, flag, and constitution. Your husband died at the moment of victory. Our Regiment with the Brigade had been ordered forward by Genl. Burnside to advance to the Bridge where the rebels were posted in strong force. They were the Brigade of sharpshooters called "Toombs Brigade" consisting I believe of Georgia, S. Carolina and Mississippi riflemen. The action lasted about one hour before poor Tom fell. He heard as he died the shout of victory. A noble death! but to you a stroke which I fear no words of mine can render alleviation. I humbly pray to my God that he will be with you in your affliction.

His grave is in the valley near the bridge, fifteen of his comrades lie there with him. I have caused an inscription to be placed over him. A final statement of his effects will be sent forward today to Washington. I enclose a lock of his hair. If you make application by letter to the Adjutant General at Washington you will get information as to the final settlement with the government. There are parties in New York who assist in procuring these settlements. If you make application to the Adjutant General Major LeGendre of our Regiment who is in New York in Broadway near Reade Street or to Elliott Shepard in Wall Street. I regret not being able to give you more information in this reference, but trust that you will find plenty of sympathizing friends who will interest themselves in your behalf. I would suggest Gen. Crooke as a proper adviser.

Again dear madame let me assure you of my deep sympathy in your loss and believe me your sincere friend.

Samuel H. Sims
Captain Company G, 51st N.Y.

Between November 7 and 15, the 51st took part in engagements in Virginia at Sulphur Springs, Jefferson, Sulphur Springs again, and Fayetteville. The regiment sustained no casualties.

13 MILES NORTH OF CULPEPPER COURT HOUSE, VIRGINIA
JEFFERSONTON VILLAGE, VIRGINIA
NOVEMBER 11, 1862

Dear Sister,

We are now encamped at the above named place. I understand that we are nearer to Culpepper than any other of our troops. With the exception of our reconnoiters we have everything quiet. Yesterday our regiment drove the rebels from a point about two miles south of our camp. [General Alfred] Pleasonton with his cavalry, at the same time, was engaged with the enemy cavalry about 3 miles off in our right.

The weather is very pleasant in the daytime but at night we have pretty severe frosts. On Saturday last we had snow all day. The people have deserted most of the houses about the country here and those who are left are mostly secesh [secessionists]. They take the confederate money and cannot tell a bogus bill from a good one so our men have been living "high" on turkeys, fowls, butter, etc. Some men find themselves suddenly rich by having counterfeit secesh [Confederate] bills with them as curiosities, and getting them exchanged in trade for good Union money. The supply trains for our division are behind two days and we are that time short of provisions, so we have to "forage" in the country. It is either a feast or a famine in camp but we manage to get along one way and another.

I have heard nothing from home since I received Mother's letter mentioning your sickness. I write in full hope that you have recovered perfectly.

The letter accompanying this was written with the expectation that [First] Lieutenant [George A.] Porter would leave for New York that day but he has been detained until today by the uncertainty of the safety of travelling on the roads. I think he will go today.

Palin is well and in the same position as before. We are waiting to hear of the draft in New York [it would not begin until July 1863]. It is said our regiment will be filled with drafted men.

You have heard that [Major General Ambrose] Burnside is in command of the Army of the Potomac now and McClellan has gone to the chief direction at Washington. This gives us satisfaction, for Burnside is thought much of by the troops.

I have nothing more to mention only to urge the settlement of the tax account and payment to Mr. Read of the semi-annual interest which fell due Nov. 1st.

We hear nothing from the north nowadays. I have not seen a [news]paper for two weeks. We also know nothing of what the rest of the Army is doing. We have been pressing close on to the rebel retreat and have taken supper at the same fires lit by the rebels at breakfast.

I must close for the wagon is going soon. Hoping to hear soon.

I remain your affectionate brother

Sam

In November, the 51st Regiment moved to Fredericksburg, where it would fiercely assault entrenched Confederates – at great cost – during the mammoth battle that raged there from December 11 through 15.

CAMP 51ST N.Y. VOLUNTEERS
EIGHT MILES NORTHWEST OF FREDERICKSBURG
NOVEMBER 18, 1862

Dear Sister,

We arrived here this afternoon from Warrenton Junction. I am in good health. So is Palin.

[82]

I received your letter and was very glad to hear you were well again.

We are in hopes now that under [Major General Ambrose] Burnside [just appointed to command of the Army of the Potomac] something decisive will be done towards closing the war. We have been marching from place to place through Virginia since the latter part of October, the time we left Pleasant Valley, Maryland. Our Brigade has been in the advance and we have had two skirmishes with the rebels with success both times. At Warrenton Springs they attempted to capture our [supply] trains as we were marching away to Fayettesville but our artillery returned and drove them away. Palin is now acting as Lieutenant in my Company. I expect he will soon get his commission. He likes it very well.

I hope now that the elections being over the Politicians of the north will keep still and let the government work in peace. The Army is disgusted with the conduct of political men north and many feel as though they did not care how the war should end. But as we advance the old feeling returns and confidence is great in our ultimate success.

The country through which we pass is entirely impoverished and we have to depend on our wagons for "grub." Under the "regulations" this can only be, hard bread, coffee and sugar, salt and salt pork. We drive our fresh beef and kill as we want it. I relish the rations, poor as they are, my "Darkey" [his African-American servant] carries a frying pan and we fry the [hardtack] crackers after soaking in cold water [to soften them up]. As a general thing we have but two meals a day while marching. When we encamp over a day or two we eat all the time that is, if we can get anything. I haven't eaten a vegetable of any kind in a month. The nearest to a vegetable we can get is "persimmons" which are now ripening but the reb[el]s have the first pick of the ripe ones, and what we find goes a long way especially if they are a little green.

To-morrow we shall start again, I suppose to Fredericksburg. The plans of Gen[era]l Burnside of course we do not know, but I do not think he will let us lay idle long, nor do we wish to, for all would rather proceed to work at once.

The weather the last few days has been slightly wet but the roads are in good condition for our business. I saw Henry Brown in the fourteenth Brooklyn the day before yesterday he is well they were at Fayettesville. Money is of no use here. What few people we find who have anything to dispose of would rather exchange for coffee or salt. I have no more of importance to speak of excepting to express the wish to hear from you and the children, also as to the settlement of the tax account, also Mr. Reads interest. Sammy, Lucy and Henry must write, Henry making his mark. So I will close with wishing you all to keep in good health and spirits.

Sam

Sammy will be eleven round years old before this letter reaches you. How the time flies!

Heavily engaged at Fredericksburg from December 11 through 15, 1862, the 51st suffered severe casualties: 12 enlisted men were killed and 6 mortally wounded; 5 officers and 50 enlisted men were wounded but recovered, for a total of 73 casualties. On December 13, the 51st was in the midst of the Federal phalanx that charged uphill across open ground in front of the Confederate stone wall atop Mayre's Heights; many of its casualties at Fredericksburg were suffered there.

On December 16, 1862, Colonel Robert Potter, commanding the 51st New York, praised Captain Sims's conduct in his report from Fredericksburg, Virginia, noting his "coolness and bravery" commensurate with the regiment's "well-earned reputation for gallantry."

In the letter below, Captain Sims writes to Mary S. Byram to inform her that her husband, Private John J. Byram of Sims's Company G, has been killed at Fredericksburg. A native of New York City, Byram was 5' 8¾" with hazel eyes, dark hair and a fair complexion. A bookkeeper by trade, he served in the 84th New York Infantry (familiarly known as the 14th Brooklyn) early in

2nd Hr to widow

the Civil War, then re-enlisted as a private on August 19, 1862, and mustered into the 51st New York that same day. He was 36 years old when he died. A year after his death, his widow applied for a government pension and received a modest monthly payment for the rest of her life from the United States government for her husband's sacrifice.

CAMP OF THE 51ST NEW YORK VOLUNTEERS
NEAR FALMOUTH, VA.
DECEMBER 19, 1862

Dear Madame,

It has become my most painful duty to notify you of the death of your husband which occurred at the battle of Fredericksburg Dec 13th.

I sincerely trust that you will be able to bear this sad news, and that a knowledge of the manner of his death may help to alleviate a pang in your sufferings.

Our Regiment with the Brigade attacked the Rebel works early in the afternoon of Dec 13th. We had reached the further-point-gained by any of our troops after passing through a fearful fire of artillery. We laid near the brow of a small hill, delivering and receiving a terrible fire of muskets. Five of our color guard had been either killed or disabled. The color [flag] was falling the fifth time when your husband caught it. He bore it until a shot struck him in the head. He was pointing at a large rent in the flag and was saying "See where our flag is struck again." These were his last words, his death was instantaneous. He was buried near the field Dec 17th by a fatigue party from our side.

I must now tell to you of the esteem in which your husband was held by all of the officers. He joined us in Pleasant Hills Maryland and obliged cheerfully the fatiguing marches to this place. Our duties have been very severe but John has never uttered a complaint – although he suffered a good deal from severe sore feet. In the last great Battle he was noticed and praised by all who saw him. His heroic death has won a place among the list of the many noble names who have bled to save our country.

My duty is now to forward a final statement of John's death to Lorenzo Thomas as Adjutant General of the army. This is to effect a settlement of his affairs with the government.

Believe me dear madame to be sincere in sympathizing with you in this great bereavement.

Praying that God in his mercy may assist and strengthen you and grant you resignation.

I am sincerely your friend.

Samuel H. Sims
Capt. Co G 51st N.Y.

Any further information I can give upon your requesting will be promptly rendered.

S.H. S.

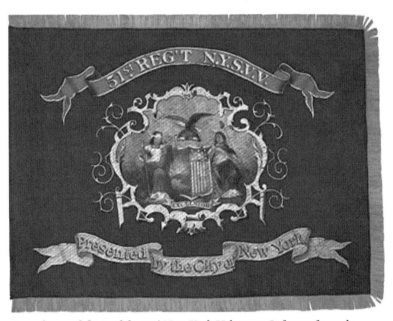

One of several flags of the 51st New York Volunteer Infantry from the Civil War. Courtesy of the New York State Military Museum.

CAMP OF 51ST NEW YORK VOLUNTEERS
NEAR FALMOUTH, VIRGINIA
JANUARY 3, 1863

B.F. Howes Esq.

Dear Sir,

Your favor of Dec 29th has reached me.

I regret to say that it is impossible to procure the remains of Byram. I would use every endeavor to that end if there was any possible chance of success. There was one of my men in the burial party and I gave him instruction to find those of my company if he could, and place a mark over the graves. He reported on his return that he could not find them. The burial party they relieved had buried all of our regiment who fell. The graves are near where the men fell. There must have been nearly six hundred dead buried in a space of three hundred yards long. A number of gentlemen have been here to recover remains of friends and but few have succeeded in finding their subject, most have returned disappointed.

At the time Byram met his death a piece of the color he held was shot away and was picked up by Sergeant McReady of my company. I enclose it to you. This color is entirely used up and I believe Colonel Potter is going to send it home to the city authorities from where we received them. To Mrs. Byram they will have a melancholy interest but sir, there are but few men but would envy the death that my brave friend met.

Praying that God may bless his poor wife

I am sincerely yours
Samuel Sims
Captain 51st N.Y.

After suffering the hardships of Major General Ambrose Burnside's ill-fated "Mud March" in late January, the 51st Regiment established winter quarters near White Oak Church, Virginia. 1863 was a quiet year for the 51st. That year, none of its men were killed in battle and only two were wounded. Captain Sims spent much of the year away from the 51st. On February 1, at the camp of the 51st Regiment near Falmouth, Virginia, just days after the "Mud March," he requested sick leave of ten days; his request was granted by Colonel Robert Potter, commanding the regiment. On March 5 he was given command of the 51st Regiment as its acting major. Three days later, Sims was serving as field officer of the day in Newport News, Virginia, for the headquarters of the Second brigade, Second division, 9th Army Corps, then commanded by Brigadier General Edward Ferrero – who had helped organize the 51st and served as its first colonel.

In April, Captain Sims was sent to Lexington, Kentucky, to recruit, and in May he was detached from the 51st to sit on court-martials convened at Crab Orchard Springs and Lancaster, Kentucky. In August, he was promoted to acting colonel and in September he was sent by order of Major General Ambrose Burnside to the Rikers Island Draft Rendezvous in New York Harbor to recruit. He remained there until December 4, when he accompanied his enlistees to the camp of the 51st and rejoined it.

CAMP 51ST NEW YORK VOLUNTEERS
NEWPORT NEWS, VIRGINIA
MARCH 8, 1863

My Worthy Comrade (Captain William Hunt, Patent Office Hospital, Washington, D.C.) – [William Hunt had served with Captain Sims in Company G of the 51st and was wounded at Fredericksburg; he was at the Patent Office, which had been converted into a hospital for soldiers, for treatment of his wound. After recovering, Hunt served as a Naval officer, commanding two gunboats; after the war he worked as a watchman in that same Patent Office building, until his death in 1898]:

My anxiety to hear from you was relieved last evening by the receipt of your letter of the 4th instant.

I have passed your letter from one to another of our officers and men, and all of them join with me in testifying sympathy and deepest respect for you, as being one who has added an interesting chapter to the history of our regiment. It is now sweet Saturday night, sacred to "sweethearts and wives." So, as we gather round to "splice the main-brace," thoughts of absent comrades are called up, and hearts are warmed up in recounting their deeds. For myself, let me thank you the kind wishes expressed in your letter. Receive in return my earnest wishes for your speedy recovery from your severe wound, and also the near reality of your hope to soon tread the pathless sea in a "right little," "tight little," sea-boat of your own, as you DESERVE, if ever man deserved anything. The method you adopted to prove your devotion to our dear country's cause will yet bear to you its proper fruit.

We are getting along first-rate at Newport News. The Regiment is in good condition. We have new tents for the men, and a model camp. There is not a sick man in the regiment! In short, we are sailing with a fair wind, and every thing is taut.

Of our comrades wounded in the battle with you, [John] Griscom has returned; [Henry] Gaynor is in hospital in Rhode Island. A brave man in a brave place, for it has furnished a Burnside and Hunt for freedom's cause. Lowery [John Loughry], I believe, is till in Washington with [Amos] Vleit. Colonel [Robert] Potter is sick in New York. Probably he will not join us in a less time than three weeks.

We have been presented with a new flag by the city of New York, and had a grand time in celebrating the event. But the hearts of our brave men cling more to the old color, baptized in the life's blood of so many devoted men, who pledged themselves to always bear it aloft in honor.

My dear captain, if God spares us to outlive the war, one of my first wishes shall be to meet you beneath a pennant of your own, to recall the past events of our cruise through the poor old State of Virginia, and take a cruise with you.

We have no immediate prospect of a move. Truly our men deserve the rest which we now enjoy. But, Captain, I cannot help feeling that we should be up and doing, as long as our flag does not float over the whole land.

I must now speak of your noble wife. Please remember me most kindly to her. I wish you had been born a few years older, and had married a little younger, and that your first child had been a daughter, so that I could get a chance to find a suitable partner. Please remember me to your eldest son and to noble little Benny. He has your solidity, with his mother's determination, and will prove an excellent man. I shall not soon forget any member of your family.

And now, dear friend, in closing, let me assure you that I am entirely at your service, in any way that you command.

We expect Burnside to command us again.

Please let me know of any need you find, in any way, and depend upon it I will attend to you.

McReady, Farmer, and all the names you mentioned, feel proud of you, and send their deepest regards. McReady and Farmer have both got furloughs of ten days, and start for home on Monday. Major Mitchell wishes to be remembered; also Dr. Leonard.

Hoping to hear from you soon, and that you will be on your feet, sound as ever in a short time.

> I remain, your sincere friend and sympathizer,
> Saml. H. Sims
> Capt. Co G, 51st N.Y.

In the letter below, Samuel A. Sims, age 11, writes from his Brooklyn home to his father, Captain Samuel H. Sims, off at war:

BROOKLYN, NEW YORK
MARCH 13, 1863

My Dear Father,

I think by this time you will be expecting a letter from me well here is one already for you to read Aunt Lucretia has received your letter. I do not think there was much skating this year. We had more snow. I will relate an incident that happened at our School with respect to the Snow One day as I went to school after dinner I got up to the lot by the side of the school and I could not see any of the boys well I played at snowball as usual until the bell rang so I went up stairs and took my seat. I noticed that there was no boys in the school and I could not tell where they was gone until Mr. Taylor said that they was all gone snowballing up Flatbush Ave out of the sound of the bell. Mr. Taylor said they would have to stay an hour after school. I am promoted in the first division of our class. I cipher in Reduction. Aunt Lucretia has got the coat already packed up. The weather has been very cold for the few days the distance from New York to Fortress Monroe is 300 miles and the direction very nearly south the distance to Pulaski is 600 miles and the direction southwest. Aunt Lucretia has received your Carte de Visite [photograph]. I must close

from your Affectionate Son
Samuel

The 51st was soon transferred to the Department of the West and, with the 9th Corps, served in Kentucky, then arrived at Vicksburg, Mississippi, in June. It participated in the Siege of Vicksburg, and was engaged at Jackson in that same state. It then proceeded to Tennessee, where it participated in the Battles of Blue Springs, Campbell's Station, and assisted in the defense of Knoxville during the siege of that city. In December 1863, many of the men of the 51st reenlisted and received a veteran furlough, then rejoined the regiment along with new recruits at Knoxville.

WINCHESTER, KENTUCKY
APRIL 19, 1863

Dear Sister,

I received your letter – enclosing one of Lucy's at Mt. Sterling [Kentucky]. We left Mt. Sterling on the morning of Friday last (2 AM) and marched to this place about 18 miles from camp – at about 11 o'clock AM. I am glad to say that we have been at last paid off and tomorrow I will enclose some money to you for I think you must need it very much. I will also send enough to settle the bill you speak of owing to Palin's receiving his pay I am now able to do this.

I have been troubled with boils on my neck. They have got well and now I have another some where else which makes it troublesome to ride.

Since I wrote last we have had three pretty severe marches. The first was 22 miles – from Paris to Mt. Sterling [Kentucky] – which the regiment under my command accomplished in 10 hours. The first five miles of which we were hindered by our being stretched across the country each side the road as skirmishers. Our next march was to Sharpsburg a town about 15 miles north of Mt. Sterling. Starting at 2 AM we reached the place at 4 1/2 AM. The object of the quick march to Mt. Sterling was to catch Humphrey Marshall's guerrillas who were threatening the place. The visit to Sharpsburg was to the same end, but we did not find them. They do not like us. We have been called "foot cavalry" by the people here on account of our rapid marches.

The country is very rich and healthy to live in. The people are divided in sentiment but General [Ambrose] Burnside has adopted a stringent course and we have inaugurated his plan. At Sharpsburg we arrested all the Rebel sympathizers and made them swear allegiance which they were glad to do. We brought seven of the worst back with us the same day, also a lot of horses belonging to doubtful citizens. I am now acting as an aid on General [Samuel] Sturgis' staff and have quarters in the hotel in town. We have been capturing from Rebel citizens a large number of horses to mount a regiment of Kentucky Cavalrymen. Tomorrow I have to hear and decide on the claims of the late owners of the horses and expect some lively times with the business. General [Edward] Ferrero has been mustered out of the service he not having been confirmed as General. General Potter (our late Colonel) is expected to command our brigade. He is well liked and will meet a good reception when he comes. There is some talk of consolidating the small regiments. If this is done it will throw out a number of officers – perhaps I may have to go but it is said that if I do there will not be a man left in the regiment for they will all desert. Very flattering to me, of course, but I hope something will turn up to prevent the disbandonment of our regiment which has so clear a record on the list of N.Y. regiments. "A No. 1" I believe is said by the Governor himself. We hope they will fill us up again and keep all the old tried officers.

I have no more to say except I hear the singing in a Presbyterian church opposite – it sounds strange for I haven't heard it in a long time. Never in Virginia. I suppose we shall be kept on the move from place to place to scare off the thieving guerrillas. We move about like the flies in the air. Thus from town to town – moving at night principally.

On the first of May there will be due the semi-annual interest to Mr. Read. I will send enough to cover this amount.

So hoping this will find you all well.

> I remain affectionately your Brother,
> Sam

The 51st, ordered to Mississippi, participated in the Siege of Vicksburg, and was engaged at Jackson.

Milldale, Mississippi
July 4, 1863

Dear Carrie,

The long agony is over. The mail arrived in camp last night bringing me a host of letters, among them three from Carrie dated May 30th, June 8th and 13th. This happy arrival gave great life to our camp and made the eve of our "national birthday: one to be remembered by us all in this land of snaiks (sic), moschetoes (sic), flies and hot weather. I have but just time to write a short note, orders having come in to prepare to move at a moments notice. A report also has been brought in that Vicksburg has surrendered. I have reason to believe it is true. This great event occurring on this of all glorious days will make new life for our people and I should like to be in New York when the news arrives, which will not be probably known there before Tuesday 7th.

Our destination may be in pursuit of [General Joseph] Johnston, who is at the Big Black River. That individual has kept "shady" for some time back, not realizing the little preparations our corps have been making for him. If we pursue Johnston our campaign is likely to be dusty enough in more ways than one. The roads are horribly up hill and down. The dust like scotch sniff so fine. Water is scarce, and the sun! It does not need a thermometer to tell us it is hot.

Well I can get along – the letters have set me all right. Yes! I would like to take a matutinal "walk" with Carrie as a companion better than anything I know of. Woe be with the luckless worm who dare to measure himself on my fair correspondent. I can not with due sense of propriety invite you to this menagerie of animated nature unless you were ironclad. Did I tell you in my last that Lieutenant Butler was bitten by a rattlesnake in the cane brake? If not I must. He was hunting for something or another and was suddenly snapped at by what is supposed to have been a rattlesnake. This was about an half mile from camp. After reaching camp in a hurry he drank some two quarts of whiskey. Strange to say this quantity did not seem to intoxicate him in the least. The place where he was bitten swelled up and pains were felt from his hand where he was bitten, extending up his arm. In about four or five hours the pain left him and Butler was out of danger. We expect to strike tents at any moment and I must close. Thanks for your good wishes and prayers. Give my kindest regards and remembrances to all. I will take care of myself as you advise. This is our second summer in service and it is said thus more severely an unacclimated persons/ We have had a little more sickness than usual but there is nothing of a serious nature. So Carrie good bye for the present and God bless you and keep you in good health, is the prayer of

Truly yours
Saml H Sims

Letter of July 4, 1863, sent by Captain Sims to his fiancée, Carrie Dayton. He enclosed two wildflowers as a token of his love – they left these stains on the letter. The Green-Wood Historic Fund Collections.

Address Vicksburg Miss.
    or elsewhere

I keep my journal and only need time to write it up. The sketches too will be forth coming and I shall remember your prior claims here after. S.

The following letter was written on the back of the July 4, 1863 letter to Carrie Dayton. Captain Sims carried these letters into battle before mailing them.

JACKSON CITY, MISSISSIPPI
JULY 15, 1863

Dear Carrie,

I have been obliged to detain this letter on account of the want of facility to post it. We marched incessantly for six days driving the army of Johnston before us. On the 9th we arrived before

Jackson City and have been engaged skirmishing ever since. We had three days of it and were under fire pretty much all the time. Our regiment has lost but one man wounded thus far. Today we are resting. Tonight it is expected that all our artillery will open on the rebels. As I write a rebel long tom [a generic term for an artillery projectile] whistled close to our bivouac. We expect to go to the front tomorrow morning again. There has been as yet no serious engagement, simply skirmishing around the whole line. Your letter of the third July reaches me in the woods this afternoon. Much obliged to you as usual but sorry my accommodations for writing are so poor so as to give you a befitting reply. It is news indeed to hear that Gus [Carrie's brother and Sam's good friend and comrade] has reached home. I trust he is well and that his wife has improved. I am acting major again. Colonel Mitchell [of the 51st New York Infantry] is in temporary command of the 35th Massachusetts. I enclose a passion flower in this dilapidated letter. They grow wild here. This letter was in my pocket when we took position to the extreme left of the lines. I had command of four companies and drove the rebels from their position where they had an enfilading – on our skirmishers. A heavy rain saturated all of my clothes, also this letter, so you must excuse its bad looks. The rain however helped me to drive the rebels for it dampened their powder. They could not fire, and were obliged to leave suddenly. For the present I must say goodbye. I trust to come safely out of this struggle as I have hitherto. I am in good health but would like a little respite from our arduous duties. I will take first opportunity to write again and let you know the result of this investment of Jackson City.

Thanks for the stamps. Write soon, direct 9th Corps as usual, Vicksburg, Mississippi.

Truly yours,
Samuel H. Sims

Sam wrote this note, undated, likely in July 1863, in the wake of the institution of the draft earlier that month:

Write to me how the draft goes. Has Mr. Smith [Captain Sims's brother-in-law] escaped? What a fine soldier he would make on a long march with ten crackers (hard) for twenty-four hours, coffee without sugar and a chunk of fat pork.

Carrie Dayton's best photograph of her beloved, Captain Samuel Harris Sims. The Green-Wood Historic Fund Collections.

This notice appeared in the *Brooklyn Union*, probably during this period:

> Captain S.H. Sims, one of our oldest and most respected citizens, formerly of the 13th Regiment N.Y. State Militia, but now attached to the 51st New York Volunteers – one of the first regiments of Gen. Burnside's command – has returned home with a view of filling up his regiment as much as possible with Brooklyn men. A very large proportion of the above regiment were originally from our city. Capt. Sims's company wholly so. The Captain's well known military talent and gentlemanly character, warrants the hope that the drafted of Brooklyn who may feel disposed to exercise their choice, will favor him or his Lieutenant McReady with a call at the armory, at almost any hour in the day in Cranberry Street. The Captain's regiment has been in the following engagements: Roanoke, Newbern, Manassas the second, Chantilly, South Mountain, Antietam, Sulphur Springs, Fredericksburg, Siege of Vicksburg, and capture of Jackson. This regiment numbers now about eighty men, which is strong evidence of its valor, and that the regimental motto, "The 51st never yields," has fully sustained its character, for never

How to recruit

has the regiment "turned its heel to the face of the enemy."

The notice was signed, "B.M.F."

By order of August 18, 1863, Captain Sims was given command of the 35th Massachusetts Volunteers in Kentucky:

But Captain Sims was soon back in Brooklyn, once again on recruiting duty. This notice appeared in the Brooklyn Daily Eagle in September 1863:

Order directing Captain Sims to Kentucky. The Green-Wood Historic Fund Collections.

THE FIFTY-FIRST REGIMENT. – Captain Sims of the 51st Regiment, N.Y.S.V., has returned to this city to receive conscripts for the purpose of filling up his ranks. This company was originally composed of Brooklyn men, entirely. It was over one hundred strong and has frequently been reinforce by recruits. It now numbers 69 men. It was attached to General Burnside's army and participated in the battle of Roanoke Island and other engagements in North Carolina. The regiment was then transferred to the Army of the Potomac and fought at Fredericksburg and Chancellorsville. Subsequently it was sent to the West and aided Grant in the capture of Vicksburg and the defeat of the rebel Johnston. "Vicksburg" and "Jackson" are now inscribed on their banners. Testimonials of their gallantry are given by General Grant and Brig. Gen. W.S. Smith of the 1st Division, Ninth Army Corps. So gallant a company should be filled up and that speedily.

On December 10, Captain Sims was ordered to the Headquarters of the Draft Rendezvous on Rikers Island in Queens, New York, to take charge of 100 new recruits and to deliver them, assisted by several other officers, to their assignments with nine New York Regiments in the Department of Virginia and North Carolina.

On January 29, 1864, Samuel Sims was detailed by Colonel Charles W. Legendre to recruit in New York's 30th District, making his headquarters in Brooklyn. Here is an advertisement that appeared in the Brooklyn Daily Eagle on March 22, 1864, above Captain Sims's name:

NOTICE TO RECRUITING AGENTS—$10 extra hand money for rec'u!ts for the New York Regi- merts for the 9th army corps–46 and 51st N. Y. App'y for infcrmation at the Cent: al Recruiting Office of Capt. SIMS, No. 14 Myrtle avenue, Brooklyn, or 593 Broadway. N. Y. f 11 1w*

Advertisement, over Captain Sims's name, as recruiting officer for the 9th Army Corps of the Army of the Potomac, offering "cash premiums" from the Committee of New York Merchants as an incentive to enlistments.

On April 19, Sims wrote from Annapolis, Maryland, to report that he had completed his duty of taking charge of 50 recruits at Auburn, New York, and making sure they made it, under armed guard (to ensure that they would not desert), to Annapolis. In May and June he was detached from the 51st and assigned to duty at the headquarters of the 9th Army Corps, then commanded by Major General Ambrose Burnside. Meanwhile, as 1864 progressed, the 9th Corps, including the 51st, was ordered east to rejoin the Army of the Potomac at Brandy Station, Virginia, in order to take part in the spring offensive; it arrived there May 1. The 51st took part in Lieutenant General Ulysses S. Grant's Overland Campaign in Virginia, and was heavily engaged at the Wilderness, Spotsylvania Court House, and Cold Harbor. During the vicious fighting at the Wilderness, May 5-7, the loss to the regiment was 79 men, including Colonel LeGendre, commanding the 51st, who was wounded in the eye. In the just more than a month that followed, the 51st saw severe fighting at North Anna, Totopotomoy, and Cold Harbor, suffering a total of 54 casualties. By June 16, the 51st, with Sims having rejoined it, was before Petersburg, facing heavily entrenched Confederates along a line of fortifications that stretched for thirty miles. The 51st soon would witness the Mine Explosion and the Battle of the Crater that followed.

Poet and author Walt Whitman was from Brooklyn. His brother, George Washington Whitman, served as a captain in the 51st New York with Samuel Sims. Walt worked as a government clerk and as a volunteer nurse in Washington, D.C., during the Civil War, treating, by his own estimate, 100,000 wounded and/or diseased soldiers, from both the North and the South.

Here Walt Whitman describes Burnside's 9th Corps marching through the nation's capital, with President Abraham Lincoln in review, and Whitman's contact with the 51st – and Captain Sims:

WASHINGTON, D.C.
APRIL 26, 1864

Dearest Mother,

Burnside's army passed through here yesterday. I saw George and walked with him in the regiment for some distance and had quite a

Civil War volunteer nurse – and poet – Walt Whitman.

talk. He is very well. He is very much tanned and looks hearty. I told him all the news from home. George stands it very well and looks and behaves the same good and noble fellow he always was and always will be. It was on Fourteenth Street. I watched three hours before the Fifty-first came along. I joined him just before they came to the place where the President and General Burnside were standing with others on a balcony, and the interest of seeing me, etc. made George forget to notice the President and salute him. He was a little annoyed at forgetting it. I called his attention to it, but we had passed a little too far on and George would not turn round, even ever so little. However, there were a great many more that half the army passed without noticing Mr. Lincoln and the others, for there was a great crowd all through the streets, especially here and the place where the President stood was not conspicuous. The Ninth corps made a very fine show, indeed. There were, I should think, five full regiments of black troops under General Ferrero; they looked and march very well. It looked funny to see the President stand with his hat off to them just the same as the rest as they passed by – then there were Michigan regiments, one of them was a regiment of sharpshooters partly composed of Indians – then there was a pretty strong force of artillery – and a middling force of cavalry – many New York, Pennsylvania, Massachusetts, Rhode Island, etc., regiments – all except the blacks were veterans, seen plenty of fighting. Mother, it is very different to see a real army of fighting men, from one of those shows in Brooklyn, or New York, or on Fort Greene. Mother, it was a curious sight to see these ranks after ranks of our dearest blood of men, mostly young, march by worn and sunburn and sweaty with well worn clothes and thin bundles and knapsacks, tin cups and some with frying pans strapped over their backs, all dirty and sweaty, nothing real about them except their muskets, but they were all as clean and bright as silver, marching with wide ranks and pretty quickly, too – it is a great sight to see such a great army – twenty-five or thirty thousand – on the march – they were all so gay, too, poor fellows; nothing dampens their spirits. They all got soaked with rain the night before. I saw

Fred McReady and Captain Sims and Colonel LeGendre, etc. . . .

– Walt

Elliott F. Shepard (1833-1893) was a lawyer, banker, and newspaper owner. When the Civil War began, he was appointed aide-de-camp to New York State Governor Edwin D. Morgan. In that capacity, he helped organize the 51st New York Volunteer Infantry; it was known as the Shepard Rifles in his honor. In September 1861, he presented the 51st with a fine stand of flags to carry into battle. Working as the commandant of the Elmira Depot, he recruited 47,000 men to fight for the Union. He held the rank of colonel during the Civil War. When President Abraham Lincoln offered to promote him to brigadier general, Shepard declined the honor in deference to those officers who had served in the field. After the war, he organized the New York State Bar Association and was its first president. In 1888, Shepard purchased the *Mail and Express* newspaper and devoted much of his time to running it. He was described by the *New York Times* as "often amusing but always in earnest."

Law Offices of Elliott F. Shepard
16 Wall Street, New York
June 27, 1864

My Dear Sims,

I was glad to hear from you by yours of the 23rd. My heart has been greatly grieved by the losses our brave boys have encountered. Colonel [Charles] Le Gendre is here [having been wounded at the Battle of the Wilderness on May 6, 1864] with his eye all patched up. [First Lieutenant Frederick] McReady's father was in to tell me that he was in the Mansion House Hospital in Alexandria [Virginia. McReady also was wounded at the Wilderness on May 6]. And this morning the Sergeant Major [John Rigby, also wounded at the Wilderness on May 6] is resting in my office, with his abdomen all stopped up, and a ball lying against his hip bone where it can't be reached. (I am going to try to get him his pay & balance of his bounty) and C. N. Potter brought in a letter from the General – and I shall go to see McKibben this P.M. Thus the 51st is ever around me, and I am too happy if I can do anything for any of them. Of course, I will accept any duty in regard to the "Bride of the Regiment" [a reference to the battle flag of the 51st New York Volunteer Infantry, the "Stars and Stripes"] that it is wished I should.

Elliott F. Shepard, patron of the 51st New York Volunteer Infantry, in his Civil War uniform.

If your present duty at the Headquarters of the glorious 9th Corps gives you a little more leisure, I hope you will improve it to my liking by writing me often, and fully about the immortal and glorious 51st. It was not necessary for me to be assured by you that you had kept up your reputation as a regiment – you already know that I consider that name a name for time and for eternity – as I took occasions to tell the world at the banquet at your reception.

Give my best love to your comrades – and tell them to write to me. Take good care of yourselves – for your lives are more valuable to the country than your deaths could possibly be. Do not let any ill-considered railing of others prevent you using the spade for defense when it can be so used [this is a reference to entrenching and the building of defensive fortifications with shovels, an increasingly-popular technique, as the war progressed, to protect the soldiers from the enemy]. An officer's duty is not to destroy, but to save life. I am sorry for D. Bird [Dr. Francis W. Bird of the 51st, who had been captured on May 31, 1864]. They will hardly send him to Charleston – eh?

The Committee for Recruiting the 9th Corps are willing to go to work again, if General Burnside desires it. But we have not had a word from him, and do not even know that he likes what we have already done.

June 28th. I saw [Gilbert Hunt] McKibben yesterday afternoon at his father's in West 31st Street. He seemed comfortable and to be doing well, although he cannot yet speak, or take any solid food. He lost seven teeth from the left upper jaw, and the doctor says his only source of danger now is from hemorrhage of the throat – that that will be past in ten days. He saw me, though he is not seeing anyone yet. If you see General Potter, please tell him about Kibbie. I shall send him fruit, wine, etc., as I have already. I hear [Lieutenant Colonel R. Charlton] Mitchell is wounded and in hospital – give my love to him, and tell him I hope he will speedily recover.

What do you think of this present campaign? What does that Rebel [General Robert E.] Lee think of General Grant?

Very truly your friend,
Elliott F. Shepard

Can I send you anything that you want?

By order of July 2, 1864, issued by Major General Ambrose Burnside, commanding the 9th Corps, Captain Sims and three companies of the 51st were relieved or their headquarters' duties and detailed back to the 51st.

As Captain Sims and tens of thousands of others awaited the call to battle at Petersburg, he turned to art to pass some time. In 1888, long after the war, it was reported that Major David F. Wright, who served with Sims in the 51st Regiment, possessed a small cast of the head of Major General Ambrose Burnside, made by Captain Sims from clay taken from the Petersburg mine. That mine, after it was sprung, launched the Battle of the Crater – in which Captain Sims was killed.

CAPTAIN SAMUEL SIMS
NEAR PETERSBURG, VIRGINIA
JULY 5TH 1864

Dear Sister,

I have not written for quite a while and I judge you have not for the very best reason that I have had no letter in sometime. Palin and I are both well. I saw Charlie last week [Sam's younger brother had enlisted in August 1862 in the 48th New York, and was now at the front in Virginia. He served through the Civil War and mustered out in June 1865], he was well.

Our duties are in front again we having been relieved from "Guard" and "Engineer" duty at the special request of General Potter. Yesterday the 4th [of July] was celebrated here by firing of muskets, and a few cannon and mortars added to the observance. There was a slight difference to the New York celebration in our having lead and iron from the muskets, cannon and mortars. In the midst of the noise of the celebration unseen agents were bidding – whist whist, and similar noises about us. I suppose the celebration was observed in N. York as usual, and while lying in our [rifle] pits yesterday imagine the scenes likely enough in the North the difference from those with which we were surrounded for some days anticipations were that we should have a lively fourth of July as it was the [first] anniversary of the [Confederate] surrender at Vicksburg [Mississippi] but everything was as usual. The same amount of picket firing which in our corps front has been chronic, never ceasing night and day. I write within short range of the rebel lines – and am seated in a "bomb proof" which is a hole dug in the side of a bank. All night it has been pop pop bang etc. sometimes much, and then less. Operations in front of the other corps are more quiet, there is but little or no firing going on. It is confined altogether to us. I suppose because we are so close to the enemy. There is little damage done however, the losses of men are very small on our side. Both the enemy and ourselves are strongly entrenched and it is difficult to hurt anyone in the front here. There is as much or more danger in the rear by the balls flying over the away beyond us. The plans of General [Ulysses S.] Grant of course I do not know but things look like a long siege of this place. Perhaps a flank movement may be made again. Tonight we go back to our camp for rest. The duty is for 48 hours then relief for 48.

Palin has a little detached breastwork made of sand bags in a ravine. Company G is with him there. I am in command of the whole regiment Major Wright holding on to his engineer arrangement until he gets further orders.

The weather is pretty warm now. We are well supplied with rations. The Sanitary and Christian Commissions send us a good many luxuries. Living, that is <u>eating</u>, is all we could wish for.

What we need most is the end of the campaign. The end of the campaign however must be the end of the war so I suppose we must be content and have our campaign go on so as to get sooner at the end.

Have you seen Mr. Ray, 51 Walker Street New York about my state pay. Our paymaster has not made his appearance yet.

Write soon and let me know how you all get along. Lieutenant McReady is home you might see him, he was wounded in the hip, at the Wilderness. He lives at Mr. Wheelers – in Schermerhorn Street near Smith [Street] – in one of two or three frame houses.

I send love to all and I trust that you will not fret about us everything is for the best. God bless you all - is this wish of your.

Brother

Sam

I think I shall have opportunity to write tomorrow so I will answer Lucy's letter. S.

After elaborate Confederate fortifications at Petersburg, Virginia, halted the advance of the Union's Army of the Potomac, Pennsylvania miners, serving in the 48th Pennsylvania Infantry, volunteered to dig a mine under the Federal positions, extending some 500 feet to the nearby Confederate lines. They were granted permission to do so and began digging in late June. The plan was then to fill the chamber at the end of the Mine with gunpowder and explode it, blowing a hole in the Confederate line and creating a gap through which Union troops, positioned in anticipation of the explosion, would rush. Captain Sims, serving in the area where the Mine was being dug, and commanding one of the regiments that was positioned to rush forward upon its explosion, undoubtedly knew of the plans; this is "the movement" he refers to below.

Camp Before Petersburg, Virginia
July 27, 1864

Dear Mother,

All of my previous letters have been addressed to Lucretia although I intended them for all at home. This one I will address to you, so you may not think I slight you.

I saw Charlie yesterday. He came up to our camp - Charlie is well, so is Palin. The usual firing continues along our front, so we are almost indifferent to it. There has been a movement of the 2nd Corps across the river some miles from here, and word reached us this morning, that the movement was a success. Matters in our immediate front seem to be approaching a crisis, certain preparations are nearly complete, and the next forty-eight hours are likely to be of great moment.

Our corps will be active and prominent in the [anticipated] movement and in all likelihood, there will be stirring times, I wish to assure you all, that I am fully conscious of what might happen to me and believe that I can meet any event as you would have me.

Gilbert Hunt McKibben (1835-1920) enlisted in the 51st in October of 1861 as a 25-year-old second lieutenant. He rose rapidly through the ranks and, by the end of the Civil War, he had been brevetted a brigadier general. The wounds described above were not fatal; he would live for another 56 years. Photograph by Jeremiah Gurney & Son, New York City.

Battle flags played a key role during the Civil War. When the flag advanced, they moved forward with it and rallied around it. And the enemy knew this, making flags and the men of the Color Guard who carried them prime targets. Stop the advance of the flag and you would stop the attack. Because flags were prime targets, they got shot up and had to be replaced periodically. Such was the fate of the old battle flag of the 51st in mid-July 1864: a new battle flag took its place and the officers of the regiment cut the old flag up as souvenirs. Written on this envelope, by Captain Sims: "Pieces of the Battle Flag of the 51st Regt. N.Y Vols. Petersburg. July 16/64." The Green-Wood Historic Fund Collections.

This I endeavor to do, however, and I trust that mercies may still be continued to me, Palin and to Charlie, for your sake.

Now I feel sufficiently serious in contemplating what may happen, but it will not do for me or any other soldier to be downhearted in contemplating what may happen to me or them when movements are on foot.

I anticipate results which will go a long way towards closing the war, and the thoughts of success make me feel cheerful.

The newspapers perhaps will tell you of what I allude to in movements, so I will not mention them here, but trust to be spared to write or tell you of them.

It is quite pleasant here today, we have had some rain lately which laid the dust, but made the rifle works rather muddy, for comfort. Major Wright assumed command of the Regiment yesterday. I have had charge of it for near a month with all its business.

Give my love to all and write soon. The paymaster is very dilatory with us; most of us have near five months pay due us. I suppose he will come along soon.

I would like to be in the midst of peace again, that is – that the whole country was at peace, for I have the same feeling now as at the start of the war – we have a brave enemy to contend against and mayhap the struggle will be continued yet a long time. I pray not for the desolation caused is terrible to think of and this campaign alone has taken all the "glory hunters" spirit quite out of them.

Having faith in God, who doeth all things well, I remain,

> Your affectionate son,
> Samuel

Carte de visite photograph of Captain Samuel Sims.
He wears the shoulder bars of a captain in the Union
Army. Courtesy of Sue Ramsey.

Sources for account of
Sims' death:

Speech at monument dedication
1864 newspaper account
Ltr from maj. Wright
Description written
by Gen. W.
Whitman
1880 newspaper
article

Two letters to
editor in
Brooklyn
paper 1864

1864
newspaper
account

3 newspaper articles
re funeral in Brooklyn

The Death of "The Gallant Sims"

SAMUEL HARRIS SIMS had written his last letter. "Always in the front and never in the hospital," his luck had run out. He was killed on July 30, 1864, at Petersburg, Virginia, in the Union attack triggered by the Mine explosion at the Battle of the Crater.

Horatio King, who in 1897 would be awarded the Medal of Honor for his Civil War bravery, gave the oration at the 1888 unveiling of the Green-Wood monument to Captain Sims, and would himself be interred at Green-Wood near Captain Sims. He wrote of the final hours leading up to Captain Sims's death:

REMARKABLE COURAGE

The fight before Petersburg brought out several remarkable displays of personal courage. Two armies confronted each other with sullen and determined bravery. On Burnside's front the Confederate lines were less than 150 yards distant. A stone might be thrown from the Union parapet into the rebel earthwork. For nearly a month 400 patriotic moles had been burrowing in the ground, carrying out the earth in cracker boxes, concealing it from the enemy's view with underbrush and steadily undermining the fort of the unsuspecting foe. Night and day the work goes on, and all hearts are centered on the project which if successful will insure the capture of Petersburg and, in all probability, the fall of Richmond. The evening of July 29th is at hand, and under the doomed fort 8,000 pounds of powder lie with deadly destruction embodied in its inert mass. The fuse is laid, at early morn of the 30th of July the match is to be applied. But daylight is past, and the troops rest impatient and inquiring upon their arms. The suspense is painful. Minutes seem hours, and yet no unusual sound disturbs the peace of that July morning. At last two heroic spirits, a commissioned and a non-commissioned officer of the Forty-eight Pennsylvania, volunteer to enter the mine and learn the cause of the delay or failure. It seemed almost certain death for them to enter the tunnel. The explosion is liable to occur at any moment and blow them to atoms, but they went in.

The fuse was found defective and was speedily replaced, and ere the sun had risen high over the old hills of Virginia, the earth shook with the tremor of an earthquake, and through the earth thrown high in the air the exploding powder blazed like lightning, casting a lurid glare upon the confused mass of dismantled guns, shattered caissons, smoking camp

This half-steroview, taken on April 2, 1865, at Petersburg, shows the type of daunting fortifications that Union troops would be attacking there on July 30, 1864.

The entrance to the Mine that was dug by Pennsylvania coal miners.
The chamber at the end of the mine was filled with powder and was
exploded with fuses; the charge of the Union infantry that followed
the explosion of the Mine cost many lives, including that of Captain
Sims, and, despite initial success, was a failure.

equipment and mangled human bodies. Simultaneously
the order to charge rang out and the third division of the
Ninth Corps advanced to the slaughter. The enemy stunned,
almost paralyzed with fear, and panic-stricken, scattered in
all directions. The concentrated fire from a half hundred guns
made a pandemonium indescribable. Into the vast crater into
which the explosion had converted the fort the troops were
huddled. There was a strange and inexplicable delay, which
gives the enemy time to rally their flying forces. The hostile,
angry guns enfiladed the crater with fatal effect. The attempt
to advance is met with a courage born of despair. A general

General Horatio King, as a young Civil War officer, and later in life. The Green-Wood Historic Fund Collections.

advance of the corps was ordered. The Fifty-first has reached the breastworks. In the forefront behold an intrepid spirit urging his men forward. Waving his sword and calling to his brave boys to follow, he reaches the enemy's entrenchments and gallantly falls in a hand-to-hand encounter with his face to the foe, a martyr to liberty and an honor to mankind. Such was the fate of the heroic Capt. Samuel H. Sims, of the Fifty-first New York Volunteers.

As per a newspaper report, Captain Sims was "pierced by two Minie bullets, one in the head and one in the breast." Captain Sims was 34 years old when he died. The report continued:

When he fell, fatally wounded, two sergeants of the regiment made the most desperate efforts to carry the body, but the feu d'enfer showered upon the regiment from the rebel guns was of so terrific a character that the sergeants retired, and the body remained for three days in the hands of the enemy.

Captain Sims was lauded in death by Major John G. Wright, commander of the 51st, who wrote from Petersburg on August 8:

I have to regret the loss of Captain Samuel H. Sims, the senior captain of the regiment, who fell fighting nobly while endeavoring to check the retreat of a regiment on our right. He was an officer of sterling abilities, and he leaves behind him a reputation untarnished, which, with his fine social qualities, has endeared his memory to all his surviving comrades.

Medal of Honor Winner Horatio King's grave at Green-Wood. Note the Medal of Honor plaque, recently-installed.

Captain George Washington Whitman, brother of the poet Walt Whitman, served with Sims in the 51st New York. On August 8, nine days after the Battle of the Crater, Whitman described the circumstances of Sims's death:

Captain Sims's shoulder board; he would have worn one of these on each shoulder of his uniform. The Green Wood Historic Fund Collections.

About 9 o'clock the order was given for our Regiment to charge the rifle pits in front of us. Major Wright was in command of the Regiment, Captain [Samuel] Sims was acting Lieutenant Colonel and had charge of the right wing, and I was acting Major and had charge of the left. As soon as the order was given to charge, I jumped up on the breastworks and sung out for the men to follow me, and the way they tumbled over them breastworks wasn't Slow. Poor Cap Sims led the right wing in fine style, and just before we reached their works the Johnies [Confederate soldiers] skedaddled. Our orders were to take the works and hold them, but after we had held them for about two hours, the rebs massed a heavy force, in a ravine just in front of us, but out of our sight, and came down on us like a whirlwind, and we were forced to fall back to our old line of works. I tried my best to keep the men from falling back, but Captain Sims was killed just at this time so it was no use trying to rally the men until they got behind their old works. The rebel charge was one of the boldest and most desperate things I ever saw, but if our men had stayed there and fought as they ought, we could have inflicted a heavy loss on the enemy, before they could have driven us away from there. The rebs did not attempt to follow us beyond their works but they kept up a sharp fire on us from behind their breastworks, but as far as our losses are concerned our Regiment got off very lucky, I think about 40 killed and wounded.

Our troops in the fort held out till long after we were driven back, and several times the rebs charged right up to the bank, and some of them jumped over among our men, and went at it hand to hand, and before our men surrendered quite a good deal of fighting was done with the bayonet alone, but finally they saw there was no help for them, and they were forced to surrender, and so the fight ended each side holding the same ground as at the commencement. One of the worst things of the whole affair was, that quite a number of our wounded lay between the rebel lines and ours, and there the poor creatures had to lay in the sun, until the afternoon of the next day, when the rebs allowed us to send out a flag of truce to give them some water, but they wouldn't allow any of them to be removed until the second day after the fight when a cessation of hostilities was agreed to for three or four hours, when what few were alive were brought off and the dead were buried.

During the cessation of hostilities some of our boys went out and brought in the body of Captain Sims and it is now on the way to Brooklyn.

Good night
George Washington Whitman

Years later, on October 15, 1880, the *New York Herald* would note of Captain Sims that "[h]is was one of the few bodies of Brooklyn dead that was recovered after the fight."

On August 9, 1864, two letters to the editor concerning Captain Sims's death were published in the *Brooklyn Daily Union.* The first, signed "F.," read as follows:

The enclosed letter to a gentleman of this city is sent to you for publication, in memory of a truly good and gallant officer. The Captain was one of our oldest and most highly esteemed citizens, and among the first to battle for the Union. He was engaged in some twenty-six engagements with the Rebels, commencing at the battle of Roanoke, N[orth] C[arolina], and until the time of his fall at Petersburg had escaped wounds, although always the first and last at the post of dangerous

Captain George Washington Whitman, who wrote a dramatic firsthand account of Captains Sims's death in battle.

"The Siege of Petersburg – Burying the dead before Cemetery Hill under a flag of truce, after the repulse of the Ninth Army Corps- From a sketch by E.F. Mullen." "Frank Leslie's Illustrated Newspaper," September 3, 1864, page 376.

duty. He was among that class whose patriotism long since entitled him to promotion, but he fell as he entered the service – a Captain. Unassuming as an officer, indomitable as a commander, affectionate and devoted as husband and father, true and loyal as a citizen, he fell a martyr to the noblest and most righteous of causes.

The following letter was written "near Petersburg" on August 3, 1864, by "J. Stuart" – Captain John Stuart of the 51st, who enlisted on August 1, 1861 as a first lieutenant, was promoted to captain of Company F four months later, and served with Captain Sims for almost three years. It read:

My Dear Sir: Our regiment has met with a most serious and irreparable loss in the death of our brother Captain Sims, who was killed on the 30th ult. while vainly endeavoring to rally the broken and flying troops of the Fourth Division of our corps. The battle in which he fell was the first he fought in which the tattered folds of our old regimental flag ("the bride of the regiment") floated not over him. Only a few days before the regiment took a farewell of it, and sent it to Col. Elliot F. Shepard to be by him, as the patron of the regiment, deposited in the archives of the State at Albany, N.Y. He fell like a true soldier in the act of performing his duty. In the midst of a storm of shot and shell, when others were falling back in dismay, he firmly stood his ground, and, with voice and gesture, endeavored to instill into the hearts of terrified and flying soldiers a portion of his own high courage, which not even death itself could daunt. It was all in vain – he fell: and the headlong impetuosity of the rebel charge prevented even his own devoted men from bringing off his body, which lay three days in the sun outside the enemy's entrenchments ere it was recovered under flag of truce and brought within our lines. There it now lies, preparatory to its being disinfected for the purpose of sending it to his home in Brooklyn. He was a widower and leaves three children to mourn his loss – a very great one to them indeed, for they are of that age when bereavement is felt most keenly. The Captain was formerly a member of the Thirteenth Regiment and was also, at the time of his death, a member of Hill Grove Lodge of Masons No. 540. Both of these bodies will probably turn out to escort his remains to their final resting place, it being the last mark of respect in their power to say to one whose generous heart and gentlemanly bearing were known to very many in both Brooklyn and New York. All his comrades in arms regret his fate exceedingly, for he was a general favorite and loved by all, especially by the men of the regiment, whose wants he carefully attended to on all occasions when in his power to do so. The remembrance of his simple, unassuming manners in the social circle, and his high, noble bearing upon the field of battle, will be retained in the hearts of his many friends long after his body shall have moldered into dust!

A newspaper account includes these details of Captain Sims's death and burial on the field:

He was gallantly urging his men to their fullest measure of duty, when he was shot down in a hand-to-hand fight upon the enemy's entrenchments. Major David F. Wright, of the Fifty-first Regiment, . . . saw Captain Sims when he fell. The latter was second in command of the regiment on that day and was as usual conspicuous for his bravery. After the regiment retreated they could see the body and the members of his company kept up an incessant fire over it to prevent the enemy from rifling it or carrying it away. After the battle was over a flag of truce went out and the body was found. It was brought in and buried in the rear of our lines. A wide grave was dug and the body was let down into it laying upon the stretcher, and empty cracker boxes were then built up around it for a coffin. As an indication of the love Capt. Sims' men had for him, one of them carved a wooden headstone and inked in the letters with black ink so that it was quite an ornamental affair. Permission was afterward obtained and the body was sent to Brooklyn . . . .

One final note on Captain Sims's death. Communication and record-keeping pertaining to the death of a Union soldier in battle were notoriously poor. There was little, if anything, the government did to inform families of the death of their loved one. A private organization, the United States Sanitary Commission, stepped into this vacuum, attempting to track deaths and inform survivors. But the Sanitary Commission's good faith efforts were limited by a lack of resources and primitive communications. So it was that, with his comrades of the 51st fully aware of Captain Sims's death, their efforts to maintain fire to keep the Confederates from his body, their retrieval of his body, temporarily burying it on the battlefield, and then shipping it back to Brooklyn, simultaneously the Sanitary Commission was trying to find out if Captain Sims was dead. Here is its inquiry of August 6, 1864:

"Captain Samuel H. Sims.
Co. G. 31st N.Y.S.Vols
9th Army Corps.
It is feared he was killed at the
Petersburgh Explosion; but not
certain. If heard of please
report to A. P. B. through
Rich'd Falconer."
Aug 6/64.

The United States Sanitary Commission's inquiry concerning Captain Samuel Sims. Though his comrades in the 51st had witnessed his death, the recovery of his body, and his burial on the field, the Sanitary Commission – with limited resources and primitive communications, had yet to confirm it.

[121]

Colonel John B. Woodward of the 13th New York State Militia. His *Biographical Memoir* is one of the most humorous accounts of service during the Civil War. He clearly had a fondness for Captain Sims, with whom he had served in the 13th, and led efforts to arrange Captain Sims's funeral and to provide financial support to Sims's orphaned daughter, Lucy. Woodward would go on to serve as a major general in the New York State National Guard and as president of the Brooklyn Institute, today known as the Brooklyn Museum. The Green-Wood Historic Fund Collections.

CHAPTER 6

Into Green-Wood's Ground

SOON AFTER Captain Sims's death, three notices appeared together in the Brooklyn newspapers. The first reported Captain Sims's death on July 30 "in the assault upon Petersburg" and invited "relatives and friends of the family" to attend his funeral on Wednesday afternoon, August 17th, at 2:00 o'clock at Reverend Mr. Bartlett's Church, Elm Place near Fulton Avenue. A separate "Masonic Notice" invited members of the Hill Grove Lodge and other lodges to attend Sims's funeral. And a third notice, issued by Colonel John B. Woodward and Lieutenant Colonel Robert Woodward, ordered the commissioned officers of the 13th Regiment, National Guard of the State of New York – the unit Samuel Sims had served in early in the Civil War, to meet at 1:00 p.m. at the Brooklyn City Armory "in full uniform, wearing the usual badge of mourning" on the 17th to act as an escort at the funeral.

The notice continued, in tribute:

> Captain Sims was formerly a member of this Company (B Company, 13th Regt.) and during the tour of duty in 1861, a 2d Lieut., returning he raised a Company in the 51st Vols., and commanded it during all the campaigns in which the 9th Army Corps have been engaged, viz: Roanoke Island and North Carolina; the Peninsula; Pope's Campaign; Antietam; under Grant at Vicksburg and Jackson; and lately with the Army of the Potomac from the Rapidan to Petersburg, where he was killed in the late unsuccessful assault on the 30th July.

Captain Frederick A. Baldwin, of the 13th Regiment, Company B, invited all members of that unit to join his company in paying their respects: "The distinguished services of this gallant officer demand that all possible honor should be shown on the occasion of the last services permitted us to render him." Captain Baldwin would soon serve as guardian of Captain Sims's orphaned daughter, Lucy.

This appeared in the *New York Times* on August 17, 1864:

> **Funeral of Capt. S. H. Sims.**
> The funeral obsequies of Capt. SAMUEL H. SIMS, of the Shepard Rifles, Fifty-first Regiment New-York Veteran Volunteers, will take place from the church of Rev. WM. ALVIN BARTLETT, in Elm-place, Brooklyn, to-day, the 17th, at 2 o'clock. The escort will be the Thirteenth Regiment National Guard. The procession will be joined in by the Free Masons. Let all who can, combine to pay the last tribute to Capt. SIMS, who has never been censured, but often commended in the past three years of his service, and who was one of the wisest, most courageous and best of men and officers.

Sims was described in the *Brooklyn Daily Eagle* as "one of the bravest and best beloved of all the brave men who went from Brooklyn to fight the battles for the preservation of the Union" and "as brave a man as ever drew a sword." An obituary in another Brooklyn newspaper reported:

Capt. Sims had been in twenty-six battles and escaped without a wound, till he met his death gallantly leading his men to the assault through the breach made by the explosion of the mine. He was one of those men who endear themselves to all who become acquainted with them. He was an enthusiastic admirer of the military profession and was a brave and skilled officer. He was offered promotion more than once, but a strong attachment to the members of his company, and a promise he had made to stay with them, led him to decline the offers.

To honor Sims, his remains were displayed in the Governor's Room of Brooklyn's City Hall.

The church services of August 17 were reported to be of "very impressive character" in one newspaper account and "in the most impressive manner" in another. A "large congregation of mourners" filled the church. Captain Sims's mother, brother (which one is unclear), and two sisters attended. "The lady to whom the lamented deceased was engaged to be married was also present, attired in deep mourning." General Crooke, Colonel Steele of General Duryea's staff, Major Dean (Adjutant General of the Fifth Brigade), and officers from the 23rd, 47th, 52nd, 56th, and 70th Regiments attended to pay their respects.

The remains were enclosed in a "handsome rosewood coffin" upon which this inscription appeared:

CAPTAIN SAMUEL HARRIS SIMS,
Captain of Company G, 51^{St} N.Y.S.V.
Killed before Petersburg July 30, 1864.
Aged 34 years.

Wreaths of immortelle flowers decorated the coffin. A battle-scarred flag of the 51st was draped on the casket. Captain Sims's sword, cap, belt and gloves were also placed atop the coffin.

Colonel Elliott F. Shepard delivered the "most eloquent and impressive" eulogy. Most of the pallbearers had been Sims's comrades in arms: two captains from the 13th – Adam T. Dodge, Jr. and another whose name is unclear; two captains from the 51st – John Stuart and Gilbert McKibben; – and a lieutenant from the 51st – Frederick B. McReady (who had been one of Sims's first recruits in Company G). Colonel Elliott F. Shepard and Clarkson N. Potter, whose brother Robert had served with Sims in the 51st and had been promoted to general, also served as pallbearers. Lieutenant Colonel William Augustus McKee, who had served with Sims in the 13th Regiment, took charge of the funeral arrangements.

A large procession, including military officers and Free Masons, accompanied the casket to Green-Wood Cemetery, where Captain Samuel Sims was interred.

A newspaper report published the next day began by describing Captain Sims as "one of the noblest of soldiers and purest of patriots." It continued:

Headquarters 13th Regiment,

N. G. S. N. Y.

Brooklyn, Aug. 15, 1864.

The Commissioned officers of the several Regiments of the National Guard, in this city, are respectfully invited to unite with the officers of this Regiment in paying the last tribute of respect to our late brother officer,

Capt. SAMUEL H. SIMS,

of the 51st Regiment, N. Y. Veteran Volunteers, who was killed on the 30th ultimo, in the assault upon the works before Petersburg.

The distinguished services of CAPT. SIMS whilst a member of the militia, previous to the war, and the gallantry and bravery shown by him in the **26** engagements in which he has taken part, entitle him to the highest honors left us to bestow.

The officers will assemble at the City Armory, corner of Henry and Cranberry Streets, on WEDNESDAY, the 17th inst., at one o'clock, P. M., in full uniform, and wearing the usual badges of mourning.

JNO. B. WOODWARD,

Col. 13th Reg't N. G. S. N. Y.

The order from the headquarters of the 13th Regiment, issued August 15, 1864, concerning Captain Sims's impending funeral. The Green-Wood Historic Fund Collections.

He had fought under Burnside at Roanoke and Newbern, under Banks at Cedar Mountain, under Pope at Manassas 2nd, under McClellan at Antietam, under Grant at Vicksburg, under Sherman at Jackson, under Foster at Tennessee, and shared in the victories of the Wilderness and Spotsylvania and survived to give his life at Petersburg as the crowning evidence of his devotion to the whole country, and his attachment to liberty. His love for the stars and stripes was both tender and heroic and led him into danger when others thought of repose.

On December 6, 1864, the *Brooklyn Daily Eagle* reported that Colonel John B. Woodward had submitted a petition to Brooklyn's Board of Aldermen for reimbursement for Captain Sims's funeral expenses. The petition, according to the report, was referred to the Finance Committee.

Brooklyn's City Hall, circa 1865, where Captain Sims's remains were displayed. It is now Brooklyn's Borough Hall.

The envelope, addressed by Elliott F. Shepard to Carrie Dayton, which held the letter quoted on the facing page. The Green-Wood Historic Fund Collections.

CHAPTER 7

The Sims Family
after Captain Sims's Death

WITHIN WEEKS of Captain Sims's death, his fiancée, Carrie Dayton, was devoting her energies to gathering information to tell his story. She reached out to Elliott F. Shepard, asking him to send her a list of the battles Captain Sims had fought in. On October 6, 1864, Shepard wrote back to her:

> Dear Madam,
>
> In accordance with your requests, I beg to append a list of the battles, so far as I have been able to collate them, in which Captain Samuel H. Sims, the patriot, the hero and the martyr, took part.
>
> Some of these, like Manassas 2nd, Kelly's Ford, The Wilderness, Spotsylvania, etc., continued from two to eight days; and each day's fight is worthy of a name by itself.
>
> > Very Truly Your Obedient Servant,
> > Elliott F. Shepard

The list, which has survived, includes 25 battles across North Carolina, Virginia, Mississippi, and Kentucky.

Captain Samuel Sims, killed at the Battle of the Crater on July 30, 1864, left three orphaned children. Just over a year after his death, on October 31, 1865, his sister, Lucretia, sought appointment in Brooklyn's Surrogate's Court as guardian for those children: Samuel A., Lucy, and Henry. At this time, they were, respectively, 13, 12, and 6 years old. Her application was granted, her guardianship to last until such time as they reached 14 years of age.

Soon thereafter, on November 16, Lucretia signed an affidavit, a Declaration of Minor Children for Pension, witnessed by Colonel John B. Woodward. In support of her application, she submitted the marriage certificate of Captain Sims and Mary Ann Titus on a form from the United States Sanitary Commission, Protective War-Claim Association. Colonel John Wright, who had commanded the 51st, also submitted an affidavit stating that Captain Sims "was killed while in the line of duty."

Captain James H. Carberry of Company A, 51st New York, stated in his supporting affidavit that he was personally present when Captain Sims was killed "by gunshot from the enemy." The Surgeon General's Office confirmed that, according to its records, Samuel H. Sims was "killed in battle." The Adjutant General's Office in Washington, D.C., reported that Captain Samuel H. Sims had enlisted in Company G of the 51st New York Volunteers on August 6, 1861, for 3 years or the duration of the war, and was "killed in action in assault on the Enemy's works before Petersburg Va. July 30/64." On November 18, 1865, Dr. George V. Newcomb submitted an affidavit to the United States Sanitary Commission's Protective War-Claim Association. He stated that he had been the Sims family physician who delivered each of their three children: Samuel Austin, born November 22, 1851, Lucy Hale, born April 1, 1853, and Henry Ridgewood, born April 27, 1859.

The three orphaned children were granted a pension exactly two years after the application on their behalf was submitted, based on their father's service, pursuant to the Act of July 14, 1862, commencing back to the date of his death, July 30, 1864, and to conclude on April 26, 1875, when the youngest of the children would turn 16. The payment was $20 per month. In 1867, Lucretia Sims applied for and received an increase in the minor's pension to $20 per month, plus $2 per minor child, in 1873; the total of $26 is equivalent to $505 per month in today's money.

UNITED STATES SANITARY COMMISSION

CLAIM AGENCY,

WASHINGTON, D. C.

Minor Children's Claim for Pension

ON ACCOUNT OF THEIR FATHER,

Samuel. H. Sims

late a *Captain* Co. *G*

51st Reg't New York Vols

Deceased *July 30th* *1864*

Filed in the Pension Office,

Surgeon General's Office,

Record and Pension Bureau,

Washington, D. C., *April 10th* 1866.

Sir:

I have the honor to return herewith application for Pension, No. *122,134*

with such information as is furnished by the records of this Office, *Capt.*

Samuel H. Sims , Co. *"G"* , *51st.*

Regiment *N. Y. Vols* , is reported to this Office by

Surgeon *L. W. Bliss* as having died *July 30* , 186*4* at

Petersburg Va. *Killed in Battle.*

Paperwork for the pension application filed on behalf of Captain Sims's orphaned children.

Part of the paper trail to establish the pension eligibility of Captain Sims's orphaned children: a report from the Surgeon General's Office, dated April 10, 1866, verifying that Sims was killed in battle. The doctor who reported his death is listed here as L.W. Bliss. That is Dr. Luther Wyman Bliss, who enlisted in March of 1863 as a 26-year-old assistant surgeon with the 10th New York Cavalry. Bliss was captured on June 30, 1863, at Hanover, Virginia. In September 1863, back in Union service, he was transferred to the 51st New York – Captain Sims's regiment. He mustered out in July 1865, died in 1906, and is interred at Oakwood Cemetery in Saginaw, Michigan.

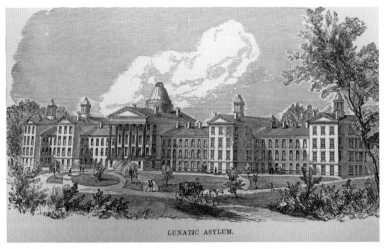

LUNATIC ASYLUM.

The Kings County Insane Asylum, circa 1870. The Green-Wood Historic Fund Collections.

Two of Captain Samuel Sims's brothers also served in the Civil War; both survived it. All three of the Sims brothers, Samuel, Charles, and Palin, are buried together in the same Green-Wood grave: section 53, lot 12512, grave 648.

His younger brother Charles (1836-1899) served as a private in the 48th New York Infantry, Company H. A native New Yorker, he enlisted at Brooklyn on August 20, 1862. At the time of his enlistment, he was recorded to be a 25-year-old native of New York City who worked as a glass stainer for Henry Bloor (just like his brother Sam) and was just over 5' tall, with hazel eyes, dark hair, and a light complexion. He mustered into the 48th that day; his service was largely uneventful. On June 27, 1865, almost three years later, he mustered out at Raleigh, North Carolina. He last lived at the New York State Home for Soldiers and Sailors in Bath, New York.

Palin Harris Sims (1827-1908), the oldest of the three Sims brothers, served as a first lieutenant in the 51st New York Infantry – the same regiment as Sam – during the Civil War. Though he survived the war, his service would scar him for the rest of his life. He would live for 44 years after his brother Sam's battle-field death. Yet, by and large, they were not happy years. The months that he spent as a prisoner of war did lasting damage to

The document prepared by Palin Sims in 1865 recording the details of his brother Sam's life. The Green-Wood Historic Fund Collections.

As per an advertisement in the 1869 Brooklyn Directory, Palin Sims was working as a plumber.

his mind and body. He, like his brother Sam, paid a heavy price for serving in the Civil War.

A native of New York City, Palin Sims was living in Washington, D.C., in 1853. He married Frances Rebecca Padgett there in 1856; she died in 1859. He was working as a plumber in Brooklyn when he enlisted as a private on September 15, 1861, and mustered into Company G of the 51st New York, the same company that his younger brother, Sam, recruited and captained. Palin was 5' 10¼" tall with a light complexion and blue eyes. He rose through the ranks: just a month later he was promoted to ordnance sergeant. Early in 1862, at Newbern, North Carolina, he was hospitalized for three months with typhoid fever. On October 16, 1862, Palin was promoted to second lieutenant. He was promoted to first lieutenant on April 20, 1864, effective upon his transfer to Company B that day. But two days later, he transferred back to Sam's Company G. Soon thereafter, at the Battle of the Wilderness on May 5, 1864, he was in command of Company G when he was slightly wounded in the face, went to a field hospital, and had his wound dressed. About a week later, he again was slightly wounded in the face, this time at Spotsylvania. He was serving as brigade officer of the day on July 30, 1864, when the Mine was sprung at Petersburg and his younger brother, Samuel Sims, was killed in battle.

On September 30, 1864, while Palin was commanding the Fifth Division, he and almost the entire 51st Regiment were captured at Poplar Springs Church, Virginia. That battle began with a Union attack in an initially-successful effort to cut the Southside Railroad into Petersburg. However, it became a Union disaster in the face of a successful Confederate counterattack. When the smoke cleared, 25 of that regiment's men were dead or mortally wounded and 8 officers and 309 enlisted men were "missing." Most of these "missing," in fact, had been captured. Palin and many of the 51ˢᵗ's officers, including Captain George Washington Whitman, the poet Walt Whitman's brother, were amongst those captured and were subsequently imprisoned at Confederate prisoner of war camps in Salisbury, North Carolina, Danville, Virginia, and Richmond, Virginia.

At Danville, Palin was held with many Union officers, including Second Lieutenant Alfred Blanchard, Jr., of the 35ᵗʰ Massachusetts Infantry. Blanchard had been captured at Poplar Springs Church on the same date as Palin Sims. About 25 years later, Blanchard wrote to describe their brutal confinement at Danville in an affidavit in support of Palin's application for a pension:

> Between three and four hundred Union officers were confined in the same rooms.... had little or no fire though it was winter season.... Lieutenant Palin H. Sims ... slept on the bare floor over an open window ... he had no covering at night and used bricks for pillows. Palin recounted that his overcoat and blanket were taken from him when he was captured – and he had none during his entire imprisonment. There were 200 men in one room; all of the windows in that room had been broken out, and there was one stove. It was in this room that he became ill.

As per Blanchard, rheumatism and ague afflicted Sims; the two of them routinely would walk the floor in the morning "to get the stiffness out of our joints." No medical attention was available. Sanitation was poor: "During the four months that we were confined in Danville we were not allowed water enough to bathe our bodies or wash our clothes though the river Dan flowed by within sight of the prison."

By February 1, 1865, Palin was suffering from a variety of ailments – kidney disease, rheumatism, fever, and starvation. He then was transferred to the infamous Libby Prison in Richmond, Virginia and finally was paroled from imprisonment three weeks later. Upon his release, by his own account "suffering from Physical & Mental disabilities," he was treated at the United States Army Hospital in Annapolis, Maryland for about two weeks. He took a brief leave of absence to return home to Brooklyn. Exchanged on March 20, 1865, so that he was free to return to service, he then rejoined the 51st at Farmville, Virginia, and "was with my company & regiment at [Confederate General Robert E.] Lee's surrender" of what was left of the Army of Northern Virginia at Appomattox Court House on April 9. Private James Prendergast of the 51st would later recall that, when Palin rejoined the regiment, he had an "emaciated appearance, and loss of physical strength together with mental weakness . . . in great contrast to that prior to his capture and imprisonment." Palin's return to service did not last long; a doctor determined

Palin Sims, wearing his medals, stands between his daughter, Eleanor, and her husband, Edward Darling, circa 1880.

Carrie Dayton's drawing and her poem. The Green-Wood
Historic Fund Collections.

that he was unfit for active duty (Palin later admitted, "I was exhausted") and sent him to a Union hospital at City Point, Virginia. He mustered out on July 25, 1865, at Alexandria, Virginia.

After his discharge, Palin returned to Brooklyn and went back into the plumbing and gas fitting business. His business partner was a soldier he had served with during the war, and with whom he had worked before the war. But after about two years Palin "finally gave up business on account of mental affliction & disease." According to the 1870 census, Palin Sims's personal estate was then valued at $2500 – a rather substantial sum for the time – about $44,000 today. Due to declining health, he had to retire completely from plumbing in 1876. He joined the Rankin Post of the Grand Army of the Republic and, likely in 1876, helped it raise money for a soldiers' home by performing in a play, the *Color Guard*, at Brooklyn's Academy of Music. But he was not well: due to "over exertion" during the run of that play "I was stricken and found myself in an asylum. I thought I was in a Confederate so called prison again." This appears to have been what today we would call a flashback or Post-Traumatic Stress Disorder (PTSD).

Confined at the Kings County Insane Asylum on December 1, 1876, he stayed there for five months. Soon after his admission, it was reported that he "has assaulted his mother, knocking her down. Talks incoherently – at times refuses to talk." Two days later, notes in the Asylum's records reported that he was "quite boisterous" and was being held in restraints – "the wristband and strap." But, by the end of the month, he was "growing better daily," conversing "freely and rationally." On March 16, 1877, after two months of doing "quite well," "friends called to take him home. There were allowed to do so."

He moved to South Hampton, New Hampshire, in 1880, where he lived for the next five years with his daughter and son-in-law, before returning to Brooklyn to live with family. In 1890 he wrote that he had "not been free from disease contracted as heretofore stated from time of prison torture, up to this time." In 1890, Palin wrote in support of his pension application, "I am not a crazy man, but my head aches at times from thinking over what I passed through – from the horrors . . . ." His "kidney complaint" dated from the months of his imprisonment; he "could not hold my water" then and "cannot hold it now." His claim to the United States government for an invalid veteran's pension based on rheumatism and severe affliction of the kidneys, physical and mental disabilities caused by exposure, starvation and other conditions he was subjected to as a prisoner was granted, relating back to 1889, under certificate 704,121.

Despite his own problems, or perhaps because of them, Palin was determined to tell his brother Sam's heroic story. In a document dated November 6, 1865, at 256 Bergen Street, Brooklyn, Palin wrote at the top: "copy of [Captain Samuel Sims's] individual record as an officer filled out by me-P.H. Sims, late 1st Lieutenant Company G 51st New York Volunteer Infantry."

He listed Samuel Sims's commissions as an officer, his service in the 13th and then the 51st Regiments, and the various battles that he fought in. It appears likely, given the similarities of phrasing between this document and the various obituaries of Captain Sims in Brooklyn newspapers in August of 1864, that Palin was the source for these details as well as the detail that Captain Sims had fought in 26 battles and had never been wounded ("health good, never in hospital"). In his notations of November 6, Palin noted that Sam "was on recruiting service during which time the Regiment did not participate in any battle." He continued with Sam's biographical details: "born at New York City, his father was Palin Sims, who is deceased. His mother now living maiden name Hannah Harris parents born Leicester England education common public school married September 11, 1849 to Mary Ann Titus, now deceased. He had three children, the oldest of whom was 13: Sam, Lucy, and Henry. At the time of his enlistment he was living at 256 Bergen Street in Brooklyn." Palin concluded: "SHS was an artist, Glass Stainer. He was a true American, loved the Union and died to save it."

Years later, Palin would return to his work on Sam's story.

During the Civil War, Carrie Dayton – sister of Gus Dayton, Sam's good friend and comrade in the both the 13th and 51st Regiments – had been engaged to marry Samuel Sims. When Sims was killed on July 30, 1864, at Petersburg, Virginia, she also made it her mission to preserve his memory – and never married. She sketched a cemetery monument with "MEMORY" on it. The cutoff column symbolizes a life cut short – before it could reach its full height, maturity. A male stands at right, his hand covering his face.

Below the sketch she wrote this poem:

> Short are the joys which friendship gives.
> When still the thought remains,
> We still may part, forever part,
> Ne'er ne'er to meet again, –
> It strikes a hard, death dealing blow,
> Upon the loving heart,
> Which time nor space can ne'er efface;
> We must forever part –
> If so't must be leave yet one trace
> One pledge of what has been,
> A friendly thought, a kindly word;
> A soothing balm may seem, –
> As time rolls on, with quickening pace,
> And cares are thick'ning fast,
> Each gentle word that's written here.
> Recalls days long since past.

In the years after Captains Sims's death, and until her own death in 1911, Carrie Dayton kept a scrapbook of newspaper clippings reporting his death, updating it with announcements of his funeral, reports of the return of the sword he had carried into battle, details of his burial, and the dedication of his monument at Green-Wood. She kept mementoes of his service: her favorite photograph of him, the peach pits he had carved for her while he served at the front, and more. She told the story of Captain Sims to her family. When she died, all of this Sims material was in a storage trunk. That trunk and its contents were owned by Aunt Estelle, descended to Stuart McPherson, and then went to The Green-Wood Historic Fund.

In 1882, Henry Ridgewood Sims, the youngest of the children of Samuel Harris and Mary Ann Sims, a bookkeeper for the North Star Boot and Shoe factory, died in Brooklyn at the age of 22. He left a pregnant wife, Anna, who would give birth later that year; their son, Henry R., would live for just less than 3 months before succumbing to tubercular meningitis. Young Henry soon would be interred in the same Green-Wood grave as his father.

On June 19, 1881, Lucretia Sims, Captain Sim's sister who had acted as guardian for his three orphaned children upon his death, married widower John Reetze. He had ties to the Sims family, having worked as plumber with Palin Sims before the war and having served during the Civil War in Sam's Company G of the 51st New York Volunteer Infantry. It was her first marriage and his second. Lucretia continued to live at their home at 296 Bergen Street in Brooklyn after Reetze, suffering medical problems, was admitted to the New York State Soldiers' and Sailors' Home late in 1895 – where Charles Sims already was living. Three months later, Reetze was transferred to the Willard State Hospital for the Insane, suffering "enfeeblement of

the mind." He died there a few months later of chronic nephri-
tis and was interred in the soldiers' lot on the hospital grounds.
On November 30, 1899, Lucretia died suddenly at the Brooklyn
home of her niece.

And what of Captain Sims's surviving children – Lucy Hale
Sims and Samuel Austin Sims? As "C.D.B." reported in a letter
to a Brooklyn newspaper in 1888, the 13th Regiment had adopted Lucy soon after her father's death, making her the "Daughter
of the Regiment":

> The members of the Thirteenth Regiment have not been
> content, however, with hallowing the memory of Captain Sims.
> They made a practical application of their regard by adopting
> his daughter, making her the daughter of the regiment,
> subscribing to a fund and expending it in her education. She
> was sent to Vassar College, and is now a teacher in one of our
> public schools.

James de Mandeville, in his *History of the 13th Regiment,
N.G., S.N.Y,* gave further details:

MISS LUCY H. SIMS, THE DAUGHTER
OF THE THIRTEENTH.

AMONG the many interesting episodes connected with the
history of the Thirteenth there was one in particular, embodying
combined qualities of pathos and romance, that testified
to the manly traits that are predominant characteristics of
the regiment. Captain Samuel A. Sims of Company G, Fifty-
first Regiment, New York Volunteers, formerly a Second
Lieutenant in Company B, Thirteenth Regiment, was killed
at the explosion of the mine at Petersburg, Virginia. Captain
Sims left a motherless daughter about fifteen years of age,
named Lucy, whom the regiment enthusiastically determined
to adopt and care for during her minority. Accordingly, in
January 1866, General John B. Woodward, then the Colonel

of the Thirteenth, formally introduced Miss Lucy H. Sims to the regiment in the Armory at Flatbush Avenue and Hanson Place, and she was adopted by the command as the Daughter of the Regiment. Each member of the organization was assessed a small sum for her support, and a committee was appointed to provide for her welfare and to supervise her education. Miss Lucy was educated at the expense of the Thirteenth at Vassar College, and after her graduation became a successful teacher in the Washington Avenue School, No. 11. During the four years that she had been the ward of the regiment upwards of $6,000 was contributed by its members for her maintenance. The committee who had the management of her affairs was composed of Colonel Woodward, Captain R. V. W. Thorn and Captain F. A. Baldwin.

The assessment for Lucy's education and welfare was $1 per annum for each veteran. A committee was established to carry out the details, and a veteran designated to be her "father." Lucy attended preparatory school, studied at Vassar College to be a teacher, and graduated with honors. She taught for many years at P.S. 11 in Brooklyn. She never married.

The November 20, 1880 edition of the *New York Herald* reported that Lucy's brother, Samuel Austin Sims, Captain Sims's eldest child, "is now about twenty-eight years of age, served in the Thirteenth and became a sergeant of a company. He is now in the flour milling business in Minneapolis, Minnesota."

CHAPTER 8

Captain Sims's Sword Returns to Brooklyn

Though Captain Sims's body was interred at Green-Wood Cemetery in 1864, his story was far from over.

In 1880, sixteen years after Captain Sims's death at the Battle of the Crater, this letter to the editor, written by James F. Steele, a Confederate soldier, was published in the *New York Herald*:

> At the battle of the Mine, at Petersburg, 1864, I was Captain of Company I, Seventeenth Regiment, South Carolina Volunteers, and in this desperate hand to hand fight, a Captain Sims, of a New York regiment (I think from Brooklyn), as he mounted the breastworks immediately before my company, was killed by Sergeant LaMott. Captain Sims' sword has ever since been in my possession, and I have frequently thought of returning it, for it should be possessed by his family as a glorious heirloom of the soldier whose conduct on this occasion was as heroic as ever illustrated any battlefield.
>
> Now, when half the North and the whole South are united in their efforts to bury animosities of the past by electing a Federal general to the Presidency, who will know no North or South in the administration of the Government, it would be unpatriotic in me to retain any longer this relic of the war. I know no surer means of discovering the address of some relative of Captain Sims than through the columns of the *Herald*. By publishing this you will probably confer a great favor on the family of a gallant Federal whose name they would not willingly let die.
>
> James F. Steele
> Cureton's Store, Lancaster County, S.C.

The very next day, the *New York Herald* reported that the letter had "attracted the attention of Major Frederick A. Baldwin of
the Veterans Corps of the Thirteenth Regiment, National Guard,
Brooklyn, . . . who, on behalf of the Thirteenth, sent a telegram
to Mr. Steele yesterday telling him to hold the sword until he
should hear further from him." That newspaper opined, "Captain Sims' sword should find its way to the family of its gallant
owner now that the brave ex-Confederate who holds it desires to
send it to them – an offering on the altar of a country knowing
no North no South. To the soldiers the war is over."

The newspaper report continued: "The 13th contacted Mr.
Steele by telegraph and both the regiment and Lucy Sims, who
was still considered a daughter of the unit, were most apprecia-
tive that the sword could now be cherished as a family heirloom.
Her uncles, Charles Sims and Palin Sims also served in the Civil
War."

On October 15, 1880, the *New York Herald* reported more
good news: "[Lucy Sims's] father's sword, a sacred relic, will
soon be placed in her possession, and the generous and manly
offer made by the gallant South Carolina soldier will be thor-
oughly appreciated by the young and old boys of the Thirteenth."

Just a few weeks later, Confederate Captain James F. Steele
carried Captain Sims's sword 15 miles from his home to an express office, from which it was shipped to Brooklyn. He wrote,
"It gives me as much pleasure to return the sword of such a brave
man as it can give his comrades to receive it."

On November 9, the *Brooklyn Daily Eagle* headlined, "An Interesting Relic: The Sword of a Deceased Brooklyn Soldier Returned to his Family by a South Carolina Officer," then continued:

The sword has just been received, and is on exhibition in the
window of the Brooks' furniture warehouse, at the corner of
Fulton and Sands streets. It is a long curved sabre, enclosed in

a rusted steel scabbard, and bearing upon the blade the words: "Stand by the Union." A card above the sword reads as follows: "Sword belonging to the late Captain Samuel H. Sims, Fifty-first N.Y. Volunteers, killed at the springing of the mine, Petersburg, Va., 1864. Returned to his family by Captain James F. Steele, Seventeenth Regiment South Carolina Volunteers, 1880."

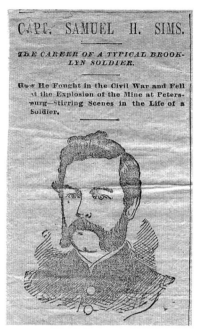

CAPT. SAMUEL H. SIMS.

THE CAREER OF A TYPICAL BROOK-
LYN SOLDIER.

How He Fought in the Civil War and Fell
at the Explosion of the Mine at Petersburg—Stirring Scenes in the Life of a
Soldier.

Lucy, at the request of the veterans of the 13th Regiment, discussed the matter of the possession of the sword with her brothers. They agreed to let Captain Sims's comrades take possession of it and to display it at the Thirteenth Regiment's Armory.

Sadly, the sword seems to have disappeared in the years since then; its whereabouts are unknown.

This portrait of Captain Sims appeared at the top of a long article about his military service. The Green-Wood Historic Fund Collections.

How did Walton know it
was Sims' grave?

CHAPTER 9

Memorializing Captain Sims, in Granite

TWO DECADES after Captain Sims's death, in the 1880s, he lay in an unmarked grave at Green-Wood Cemetery. But he had not been forgotten.

Captain Charles W. Walton had enlisted in the 51st Regiment on September 23, 1861, as a 19-year-old private, and had worked his way up to captain of that regiment's Company D and then E, being wounded at Antietam along the way. In 1886, he was walking through Green-Wood Cemetery and came upon Captain Sims's unmarked grave. Walton immediately realized that Sims deserved better; he promised himself he would not cease his efforts until an appropriate monument marked the grave of the "Gallant Sims." Walton spent the next two years raising every dollar that was needed for the erection of that monument.

In 1888, an article recalling Captain Sims's career appeared in a Brooklyn newspaper. The article, signed "C.D.B.," recounted at length Captain Sims service during the Civil War, as well as the history of the 51st New York Volunteers. It lauded Captain Sims:

> Captain Sims was a man of such marked traits of character that, notwithstanding the fact that he filled a subordinate office, his name and character is revered by hundreds who enjoyed his friendship. He is described as a man of extremely quiet and unassuming ways, but in battle as brave as a lion. In his militia service he was noted for strict and faithful attention to duty and a soldierly bearing, which impressed all with whom he came in contact.

After detailing the 51ˢᵗ's service in the 9ᵗʰ Corps, and the battles it fought at Roanoke Island, Newbern, South Mountain, Antietam, Fredericksburg, East Tennessee, the Wilderness, Spotsylvania, Cold Harbor, and Petersburg, the writer continued:

> In all these battles, sieges and marches, Captain Sims performed his part faithfully, and never receiving even a scratch until the disastrous explosion of the mine in front of Petersburg, July 30, 1864, and the assault following it, when he yielded up his life to the cause of liberty.

The account concluded:

> The colored division and finally all of the Ninth Corps were put into the battle. And it was here that our hero fell. He was gallantly urging his men to their fullest measure of duty, when he was shot down in a hand-to-hand fight upon the enemy's entrenchments.

The 1888 newspaper article provides further details of the ongoing efforts to erect an appropriate memorial at Captain Sims's grave.

> The survivors of the Fifty-first Regiment have made up a fund for the purpose of erecting a monument over Captain Sims's grave, and the responses which they have met with were most hearty and spontaneous and thoroughly establish the fact that Captain Sims was a man of no ordinary mold, for his memory is kept fresh in the hearts of his former comrades, notwithstanding the years that have flown since he fell a noble martyr to the country's cause. Captain C. W. Walton, a veteran of the Fifty-first Regiment, who resides on Schermerhorn Street, has been active in collection funds for the monument, which will cost about $550 and will be unveiled on July 30.

The committee for the monument consisted of Major Frederick Baldwin, Captain Charles W. Walton, and Captain John Rapelje.

On September 17, 1888, the Sims Monument was unveiled at

Green-Wood's Cedar Dell. Carriages transported ladies, many of whom were in attendance, from Green-Wood's main gates to Captain Sims's grave. Sergeant William Welch, who had served with Sims in the 13th Regiment early in the Civil War, had told his comrades that he would meet them at Green-Wood's main gates half an hour before the ceremonies were scheduled to begin. He would have badges for each of them to pin to their clothes. Sadly, Welch did not make it to the dedication of the Sims Memorial; he died just days earlier.

The ceremonies began, despite rain, at 4:00 p.m.. A reporter for the *New York World* described them as solemn and impressive. The monument, about to be unveiled, was draped in the Stars and Stripes. Two American flags bracketed a framed photograph of Captain Sims that rested against the footstone of his grave. On the flag that covered his grave rested the sword he had carried into his last battle – the sword that had been taken from him upon his death by the Confederate Steele, then returned to the Sims family in 1880.

After the crowd gathered at the grave, drummer Jesse W. Mills beat the assembly. Drummer Mills was not just some drummer who had been hired to supply a bit of music – rather, he was Captain Sims's drummer, having served under Sims's command in his companies of the 13th and 51st Regiments. As the Civil War had gone on, many long months after Mills had drummed Captain Sims's Company G into battle at Newbern, Mills was twice wounded in action and twice captured; he escaped from one captivity and was exchanged after the other. After the war, Jesse married Mary Ellen Hopkins and worked as a hatter. He served in the 23rd New York State Militia after the war for more than 23 years and was active in the Grand Army of the Republic, a fraternal organization for Civil War veterans. He later moved to New Jersey, then to Florida, where he died

Drummer Boy Jesse Mills's Green-Wood gravestone. His grave was unmarked until just a few years ago, when Green-Wood's Civil War Project successfully applied to the Department of Veterans Affairs for a gravestone; it was installed by Green-Wood's staff.

in 1937, at the age of 91. Mills was interred at Green-Wood, in section 25, lot 7405 – not far from the grave, and monument, of Captain Sims – and next to his wife, Mary Ellen.

General Horatio C. King, who would receive the Medal of Honor nine years after this ceremony for having helped to repulse a Confederate attack at Dinwiddie Courthouse, Virginia, on March 31, 1865, and leading a countercharge, and would himself be interred at Green-Wood in 1918, gave the oration at the unveiling of the Sims monument.

King noted that "within the reach of my voice" were the graves of five named Civil War veterans. He continued: "Comrades, beneath this monument reposes the dust of a man, brave without bravado; tender as a woman; true as steel, as honest as he was true and beloved for all those traits which unite to make a well-rounded character." He noted Captain Sims's unassuming manner and "lion-like bravery."

King made reference to Captain Sims's sword:

On the walls of the veterans' room in the armory of the Thirteenth Regiment, of the National Guard of New York, hangs a rusty sword. The scabbard is tarnished by time and indented by rough usage. The blade is rusted and the external appearance of this disfigured weapon does not justify the honor conferred upon it. But around it clusters the memory of a brave man, a heroic death and a generous recognition by a conquered foe.

Two of the greatest armies the world ever saw, with sullen and determined bravery, confronted each other before Petersburg.... Captain Sims was a typical volunteer soldier, one of that great body of patriotic citizens who, ignoring every other claim of affection, self-interest and the demands of domestic life, responded with alacrity to his country's call at the very outbreak of the war.

Invitation to the unveiling of the Sims Monument (at left) and the program for the unveiling (right). The Green-Wood Historic Fund Collections.

General King quoted a tribute to Sims, written by one of his comrades in arms:

Captain Sims I considered a man of uncommon ability and undoubted courage – a sort of modern Chevalier Bayard, without fear and without reproach. Such men gave tone and vitality to the service. Singularly free from vices common in camp life, his influence on the men of his command was at all times good, while by his calm, collected manner under the most trying circumstances he inspired them to do their best. To have him in command of the skirmish line when it was to be advanced was a satisfaction to every man deployed. It is eminently fitting that the surviving members of the regiment should join in erecting to his memory what at best can be but a feeble tribute to his rare merit as a soldier, his sterling worth as a man.

A choir then sang the hymn, "Nearer My God to Thee." A note on the song sheet distributed to attendees read: "All are requested to join in singing." A letter from Colonel Elliot F. Shepard, for whom the 51st New York, the "Shepard Rifles," were named, and who had been a friend of Samuel Sims, but could not be present at Green-Wood for this dedication, was read. In an 1893 report in the *Brooklyn Daily Eagle*, it was noted that "Colonel Shepard took a great deal of interest in the monument to Captain Sims and was a liberal contributor to the fund." Shepard wrote, in part:

> Among the soldiers with whom I had the honor to rank as a friend was Samuel H. Sims. Each of the nine bullets which struck him in the "imminent deadly breach" of the Petersburg mine, struck down a virtue – patriotism, bravery, coolness, simplicity, temperance, gentleness, truth, mercy, charity.

After a minister's invocation, Louise Sims, Captain Sims's only grandchild, unveiled the monument. The daughter of Captain Sims's son Henry, she had been born in 1880, and was only eight years old at the time of this ceremony. The *New York Mail and Express*, published the day of the dedication, described the monument:

The monument is twelve feet high, of granite, a rectangular pyramid in shape.

The inscriptions on the four panels of the monument are couched in simple and expressive language and show the deep regard in which the memory of their old comrade is held.

Almost 130 years later, the granite today remains in excellent shape:

The front and left side of the base. Note "OUR COMRADE" across the bottom of the front. The veterans of the 13th Regiment of the New York State Militia and the 51st New York Volunteer Infantry, both of which Samuel Sims served in during the Civil War, pooled their resources to erect this monument.

Two of the four sides of the obelisk that list the battles in which Samuel Sims fought.

Carved into the granite obelisk that tops the monument are the names of all of the battles in which Sims led his men and in which he so bravely fought.

The granite monument was made by William E. Kay, described in one report as "the marble-dealer of Twenty-fifth street" in Brooklyn; his business was near Green-Wood's main entrance, along its primary access road. William's father, Peter, had served for two years under Captain Sims's command in Company G of the 51st Regiment.

Drummer Jesse W. Mills then played the "Tattoo," "Lights Out." A bugler concluded the program with "Taps."

Sadly, on April 19, 1889 – just seven months after the dedication of the monument to her father at Green-Wood, Lucy Sims, the only daughter of Samuel and Mary Ann Sims, died from tuberculosis at her home at 1311 Dean Street in Brooklyn. Still a young

woman of only 36 years, just two years older than her father had been when he was killed in battle, she was buried alongside him, between Dogwood and Cedar trees, in a grave dug at the base of the Sims Monument. The back of the Sims Monument, which purposely had been left blank, was inscribed in her memory.

In the *History of the 13th Regiment, N.G., S.N.Y*, author James de Mandeville wrote:

The men who served with Samuel Harris Sims held him in the highest esteem. They had this carved into his granite monument: "IN LIFE/ WE ESTEEMED/THIS VALIANT SOLDIER/IN DEATH/WE HONOR HIM./WITHOUT FEAR AND WITHOUT REPROACH"

Miss [Lucy H.] Sims died April 19, 1889. She was buried in Greenwood cemetery beside her father, under the shadow of the monument erected to his memory by the Fifty-first

Regiment, New York Volunteers. In accordance with her request a panel on the shaft was left for an inscription for herself, which is now being cut at the expense of the Veteran Association of the regiment. The inscription will read as follows:

LUCY H. SIMS,
DAUGHTER OF THE 13TH REGIMENT, N. G., S. N. Y.,
DIED APRIL 19, 1889.

The inscription to Lucy Hale Sims, "Daughter of the Regiment," as it appears on the back of the Sims obelisk.

[CHAPTER 10]

Keeping Captain Sims's Story Alive

CAPTAIN SAMUEL SIMS died in 1864. Yet, his story can be told more than a century and a half after his death because his family, his fiancée, and their descendants, as well as strangers, cherished his story and preserved the objects and papers that made it possible to tell it.

Stuart McPherson grew up with that trunk, the contents of which were collected by Carrie Dayton, who had been affianced to Captain Samuel Sims. Those contents were passed along to Stuart's ancestors, who passed them along to him. He was thrilled on the day he first saw that trunk opened. And he treasured it and its contents for many years.

And Captain Sims's family kept the papers he had left. His brother, Palin, his son Samuel A. and his grandson, Kenneth, all preserved what Captain Sims had left.

Palin had served during the Civil War in the 51st New York Volunteer Infantry with George Washington Whitman. Captain Whitman wrote the most detailed account of Samuel Sims's death at the Battle of the Crater. On March 17, 1885, Palin wrote to George's famous brother, the poet Walt Whitman, to reminisce about his Civil War experiences, in the hopes of hearing from him:

1/4 to 5 a.m.
March 17, 1885
220 Washington Street
Brooklyn New York

Walt

 Circumstances, Recollections, and an irresistible will I might say, induces me to write for the purpose of gratifying you and

George as well as myself. I often see your name mentioned in the various papers, and I have your address in my Memorandum Book. Well now to the point. Let us recall your visit previous to the battle of Fredericksburg.

The Tent You and I took the rest and the memories of the scenes and the effects of our thoughts there, and since then, the various trials, scenes pleasures, hopes, fears of each us three, Walt, George, Palin, and then how we follow on, and then on the 30th Sept 1864, and then after 3 years & 15 days to be in Command on that extreme left flank, when the order came through the lips of Wright. Keep up a fire, and then our retreat, the last to retreat, and surrender, then on to Richmond and on and on to Danville, then George's absence, his return, his few remarks, and then x x our exchange, return, the absence of Sam, of Butler – - Lincoln. Oh Walt what scenes, trials we pass through life yet can we not look back with somewhat of a hope that all was for the best, that we are blessed with light, with Fraternity, Charity & Loyalty to all with Malice towards none, that it is a great pleasure for us, for you to hear from me, that you see I have a lingering appetite to let you and George know that I am still here in this mortal coil and that I desire a few lines from you, that we may at times through the great facilities of the present day correspond and now and hereafter may we hope to be able to see each other in that Celestial light vouchsafed to all mankind.

Truly Yours

Palin H. Sims

late Co G 51st New York Volunteer Infantry –

1861 to 1865

N.B. I am living with my son-in-law, his wife (my daughter [Eleanor) and their 2 children. I gave up plumbing business some time ago. I am not rich in money. Captain Sam's sword is now in 13th Regiment armory – his remains in Greenwood.

-P H S

1/4 to 7 a.m.   Walt Whitman

The preceding remarks are written with a view to further correspondence yet a few lines, your signature, might suffice and I would be pleased to hold a letter from you, one who I esteem, one who knew, my Brother,

I have had quite a correspondence with a Captain Steele late of the so called Confederate Army, who is published, [nay?] I have it in his own hand writing that his Sergeant, DeLaMott, Shot, Captain Sims. This circumstance, and confessions showing regrets &c, &c I sometimes think would be a theme for one of talent such as I believe you possess and I hope a correspondence will be happy interviews in the sweet bye & bye

P.H.S.

We have no record of a response from Whitman.

Palin continued to suffer early in the 20th century from the impact of his horrific Civil War experiences. In 1905, his application for an increase in his pension to $30 (from $12 per month) was awarded, "caused by the toil and long confinement in rebel prisons and that in consequence of the above and his advanced age, he is entirely unable to engage in any labor of any kind; that he is without means, and has been provided for by his son-in-law and daughter, etc." Palin Sims and his son-in-law Edward Darling, with whom he lived late in life, are credited with getting the Brooklyn Heights Railroad Company to place a "stationary car" (a place to wait, protected from the elements) at Bay Ridge Avenue and 13th Street, for the use of those traveling on the Bath Beach and Bensonhurst Railroad Line.

As Palin's life approached its end, he worked at organizing Captain Samuel Sims's papers. In 1905, he wrote to his nephew and Sam's son, Samuel A. Sims. Kenneth – mentioned in the letter below – was Samuel A. Sims's son – and the grandson of Captain Samuel H. Sims:

Monday, Oct. 23, 1905
1232 67th St.
Brooklyn, NY

Sam,

Yours rec[eive]d. All glad to hear from you.

Am glad to hear that you would like to arrange the war letters for Kenneth's benefit and I believe of your own, and others.

This is what I have been doing since 1861 and I will send you as circumstances occur. With this I send a copy of one letter – his first Battle. I copied it this day. I do this for reasons – as I value all of our sayings and know they are precious to all good Union men of the days of 1861-5 and are up to date.

They are valuable, they are written, they will, and have been, commented on and be the means of supplying the trials of the mind, a fact, an evidence of what they passed through.

Your Uncle,
Palin H. Sims

As Palin transcribed the letters sent and received by Captain Sims, he made notations of their dates, sender and recipient, and initialed them.

But Palin's work would be cut short. In his later years, Palin H. Sims was known as "The Old Soldier." The following excerpt from an article in the *Brooklyn Daily Eagle* of July 5, 1908, entitled "Honors Paid Aged Veteran," captures the esteem and affection with which he was held in the Lefferts Park section of Brooklyn, and reports his death:

If the sun has ceased to shine, there perhaps would not have been greater gloom in Lefferts Park this week than when Lt. Palin H. Sims, "The Old Soldier," an honorable, brave and battle scarred warrior, who had served throughout the entire Civil War and suffered incarceration in the famous Libby Prison, breathed his last at the home of his son-in-law, Edward L.

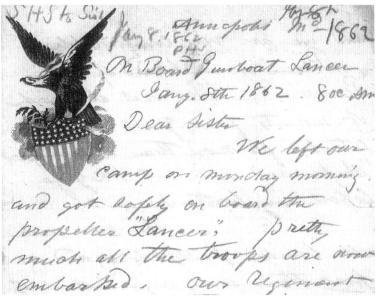

An example of Palin Sims's notations, made as he read through, and organized, his brother Sam's Civil War letters. Here he notes at the top of this letter that it is from Captain Sims ("SHS") to their sister, that it is dated January 8, 1862, and then adds his own initials ("PHS") to indicate that he has reviewed the letter.

Darling. The old veteran who was 86 years old was one of the most honored citizens of the southern section of Brooklyn and the idol of the children from whose eyes there rushed tears of intense sadness when it was announced that the warrior had answered the bugle call of the General of All.

Palin last lived at 1232 67th Street in Brooklyn.

The "Sam" to whom Palin wrote in 1905, Samuel Austin Sims, was the eldest of Samuel Sims's sons – and Palin's nephew. When his Uncle Palin died, Samuel was the only surviving child of Captain Samuel Sims, and it was to him that the papers of his father passed upon Palin's death.

In 1878, Samuel Austin Sims, 27 years old, moved from his native Brooklyn to Minneapolis, Minnesota, and went to work as a bookkeeper in a flour mill. He soon got into the banking business, where he worked for the next four decades.

Like his father before him, Samuel Austin Sims joined the local militia as a young man. The Minneapolis Light Infantry was the second oldest military organization in Minnesota, after only the Governor's Guard. In July 1879, the Light Infantry held its first drill – and that drill was commanded by none other than First Lieutenant Samuel A. Sims. On October 6, 1879, when the company mustered into state service, Lieutenant Sims was in command. He remained in charge of the regiment until February 1880, when a captain was appointed. Samuel was elected first lieutenant and adjutant of the First Battalion in 1882. He also served as judge advocate in at least one, and probably several, courts of inquiry.

On the 9th day of September 1880, Samuel A. Sims married Harriet F. King at her home in Minneapolis, Minnesota.

Harriet Kings Sims – or Hattie, as she was known – kept a scrapbook over the years of newspaper clippings. This is the cover of the scrapbook, which contained reports of her wedding to Samuel Austin Sims, the death of their baby, their visit back to Brooklyn, as well as death announcements for Samuel's sister Lucy, his uncle Charles, and others in their family. The Green-Wood Historic Fund Collections.

The wedding, according to a local newspaper,

> . . . took everybody by surprise. The company present were merely invited to spend the afternoon, and hadn't decked themselves out in all their gay plumage. They recovered, however, from the shock sufficiently to place a good many obstructions in the path of the pair, in the way of old shoes, etc.

Soon thereafter, this item appeared in a local newspaper:

> As a regular meeting of the Minneapolis Light Infantry last evening the members agreeably surprised First Lieut. S.A. Sims by presenting him with a complete and elegantly bound set of Dickens' works. It was intended as the company's wedding gift to the lieutenant who was recently married.

In February 1884, Hattie gave birth to William Dana Sims. Sadly, William died in August of that year. Once again death had visited the Simses. The family scrapbook has this poem pasted between two newspaper announcements of the baby boy's death:

ONLY A BOY

Only a boy, with his noise and fun,
The veriest mystery under the sun;
As brimful of mischief, and wit and glee,
As ever a human frame can be;
And as hard to manage as – what? ah me!
'Tis hard to tell, yet we love him well.

Only a boy, with his fearful tread,
Who cannot be driven, but must be led;
Who troubles the neighbors' dogs and cats,
And tears more clothes, and spoils more hats,
Loses more tops, and kites, and bats
Than would stock a store for a year or more.

Only a boy, with his wild strange ways,
With his idle hours and his busy days;
With his queer remarks, and his odd replies,
Sometimes foolish and sometimes wise;

Often brilliant, for one of his size,
As a meteor hurled from the planet-world.

Only a boy, who will be a man,
If nature goes on with its great plan;
If water or fire, or some fatal snare.
Conspire not to rob us of this, our heir,
Our blessing, our trouble, our rest, our care,
Our torment, our joy – only a boy.

Samuel Austin Sims, who was only 12 years old in 1864 when his father, Captain Samuel Harris Sims, was killed at the Battle of the Crater, died on November 20, 1919, in Excelsior, Hennepin County, Minnesota, at the age of 68. An obituary in the local newspaper reported that, though he had been ill for a year, the news of his death "cast a cloud over the community in which he had lived for so long and in which he was held in such loving esteem." The newspaper account concluded:

> Mr. Sims was a gentleman of refinement and scholarship. He was widely read in science and natural history as well as in fiction. He was fond of travel and had made a tour through Europe. His patriotism was of the highest and he was always proud of the long years he had spent in the National Guard. His gentle manners and kindly ways caused him to be honored by all who knew him. In his death the community loses a Christian citizen of the noblest type.

Samuel Austin Sims was survived by his wife Harriet and their son Kenneth (who had been born in 1900). Kenneth was a student at the University of Minnesota when his father died. Upon Samuel's death, the papers of Captain Samuel Sims went to Kenneth, who would preserve them throughout his life. When he died, they went to his widow. And when she died, they would wind up in the trash. But they would be saved – to help tell the story of Captain Samuel Harris Sims, "The Gallant Sims" – artist, husband, father, leader in battle, and hero.

INDEX

SET IN MILLER AND BELL TYPES
PRINTED ON ACCENT OPAQUE PAPER
DESIGN AND TYPOGRAPHY
BY JERRY KELLY